# The Singapore Letters of Benjamin Cook
## 1854 ~ 1855

Singapore, 10 January 1855

My dear Harry,

My first letter to you of a new year which I hope will bring much happiness to us, our families and our friends. Now, if I tell you that it did not start in the most auspicious way, do not take it as any prelude to future happenings. Can a New Year celebration with the Great and the Good be expected to be enjoyed? Yes, it can, but not in the circumstances under which I saw in 1855.

We had been asked to the event at the Church's house, and even my uncle, a man who enjoys a party, was none too enthusiastic but felt that there was no polite way in which to decline. Our departure from home was delayed by some mishap to the carriage, which I initially thought was misfortune as I remember the excellent wedding held there some months ago. But later I saw it as one of the few pieces of luck that evening. We finally got to the

# The Singapore Letters of Benjamin Cook

## 1854 ~ 1855

Adrian G. Marshall
Illustrations: Lim An-Ling

·LANDMARK·BOOKS·

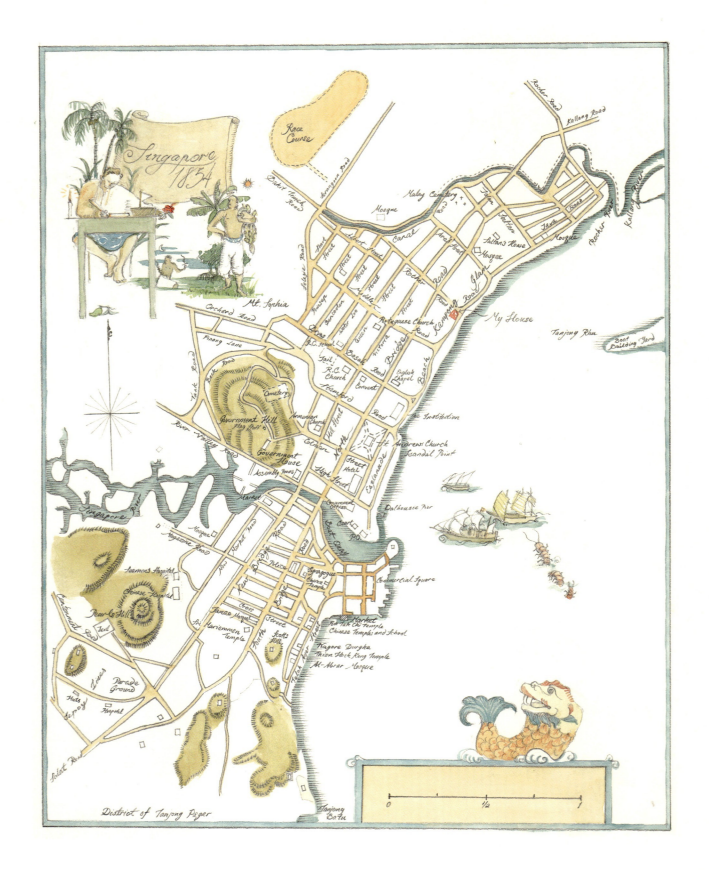

Singapore 1854

Race Course

Rochor Road
Kallang Road
Kallang River
Rocher River

Serangoon Road
Bukit Timah Road

Maly Cemetery
Mosque
John Gation Road
Java Road
Mosque

Canal
Sultan's House
Mosque
Arab Street
Rochor Road

Selegie Road
Queen Street
Victoria Street
Middle Street
North Street
South Street

Mt. Sophia
Portuguese Church
Kampong Glam

Orchard Road
Kampong Road
My House

Pinang Lane
R.C. School
Queen
Victoria
Bras Basah Road
English Chapel
Beach
Tanjong Rhu
Boat Building Yard

Tank Road
Jail
R.C. Church
Convent
Stamford Road
The Institution

Back Road
Cemetery
Armenian Church
St. Andrew's Church
Scandal Point

Government Hill
Flag Staff
Coleman Street
North Bridge Street

River Valley Road
Government House
Hotel
Esplanade

Assembly Rooms
High Street

Market
Government Offices
Dalhousie Pier

Singapore River
Mosque
New Market Road
Boat Quay

Magazine Road
Police Street
South Bridge Road
Court
P.O.
Commercial Square

Seamens Hospital
Chinese Temple
Synagogue

Chinese Hospital
Pearl's Hill
Jail
Cross Street
Fish Market
Fuk Tak Chi Temple
Chinese Temple and School

Cantonment Road
Java Mosque
Sri Mariamman Temple
Fourth
Scotts Hill
Nagore Durgha
Thion Hock Keng Temple
Al-Abrar Mosque

Sepoys Lines
Parade Ground
Huts
Sepoys
Hospital

Salat Road

District of Tanjong Pagar
Tanjong Batu

0        ½        1

# Table of Contents

Lighthouse at Cape St. Vincent

*Thursday, 27 April 1854*

My dear Harry,

At last I can write to you 'I am in Singapore'. And I can say that so far it has met all the expectations that we had together in our ignorance. Certainly, it is small compared with that vast sprawl we call our home, but its streets are as hectic as London streets and so much more diverse, and everywhere and every day seems as colourful and warm as Hyde Park on a summer Sunday. How can I describe all this to you? I will not try – not yet, not until I know it better.

Instead I will tell you something of our journey. I meant to write to you before, during all those long days ploughing over calm seas, to post it to you from 'Alexandria', from 'Aden', from 'Point de Galle', those names we had conjured with together. But the time and not the pen flew.

Oh, it seems an age since I saw you by the dock, waving and shouting as the *Euxine* slipped her moorings, yet it was but seven weeks ago. I suppose I should have felt sad to see England, with my family and my friends and all I knew, slipping away. But the ship held so much promise, the funnels pumping their thick black smoke, the paddles thrashing the ocean. Such action, such purpose! And on that first glorious day I felt only excitement. Later, when suddenly awakened by a great crash, and in the darkness not quite knowing whether I was still in my bunk or on my head or on my heels, I learned that ships and the seas on which they sail are not always benign. But then I had heard that the seas to the west of France were often stormy, and when later after a sleepless night dawn had come, and I had with difficulty dressed and staggered up on deck, I also learned how magnificent a rough sea can be. And also, thank goodness, that I was a good sailor. At least, a fairly good one! Calm weather returned off Cape St Vincent, a rocky headland crested with a lighthouse which gleamed white in the pale sunshine, and indeed that early storm was the only one we met with on all our voyage.

We reached Gibraltar on the Monday evening, but there, owing to fear of the cholera, we were quarantined, and all communication with the ship was by means of tongs and basins of water to drop the money in. In the morning light the rock was most impressive, the little town of St Roque to one side and the snow-capped Sierra Nevada rising clear and cool behind. Across the Straits to the south, Africa; Ceuta with its white flat-roofed houses set against a small hill. And so we entered the Mediterranean, the sea cut by our bows a remarkable blue. Around us dolphins played, and although we were making good time kept easily beside us.

Our next port we again reached at night. But luckily the talk of cholera had not reached Malta, and the following morning we were allowed ashore. And so at last I set foot upon a land other than England's and glimpsed a people other than Englishmen. The island looks barren, but the harbour is very fine surrounded by a pretty town and fort. Our shore leave was from 6 till 9 on the Saturday morning, and we had time to walk through the narrow streets, to visit the Cathedral of St John, brilliant with paintings and statues and the tombs of the knights, and finally to return by the bustling market. What a colourful and hectic people, and all conversing in a language of which I knew not a word!

And so on across a calm blue sea to Alexandria, arriving there on Tuesday the 21$^{st}$, thirteen days out from London. But before I tell you about the most exciting part of our journey, I should tell you a little about my fellow passengers. Amongst the English, the largest party was bound for India, some

officers and about twenty cadets, and there was also a group of officers for Alexandria. Then there was a family, the Armitages, bound for India, a naturalist, Mr Wallace, and his assistant for Singapore, a Government interpreter and three clerks for China, and four businessmen for Australia. In Malta two other Englishmen joined us, a clergyman on a pilgrimage to Jerusalem, and a government servant for Bombay. Then there were three clerks from Edinburgh going to Calcutta, a Portuguese officer to Goa, a Frenchman to Cochin China, three Spaniards to the Philippines, and a gentleman and two ladies from Holland to Batavia. So we were a party of many tongues.

One of my cabin mates was Charles Allen, assistant to the naturalist, about two years younger than me though he looks only about 12, and a nice boy, cheerful and enthusiastic. The other was one of the Indian cadets, a very superior fellow and knowingly handsome, with a fine dressing-case and jewellery, who spent much time studying either the mirror or a Hindustani grammar. Not far from our cabin two were occupied by the Armitages, Jack and his two younger sisters bound with their parents for Calcutta where Mr Armitage was to take up some government post. Jack must have been a couple of years younger than Charlie but he was a lively boy,

*Alexandra, a view from my room*

Donkey Boy

well read and full of fun, and the three of us would often talk and play together.

And so to Alexandria, only glimpsed that evening as the Company rapidly transported us to a comfortable hotel and after a long day and a good meal we were ready to retire. And the good meal was certainly much appreciated, for whatever strengths the Pacific & Orient Company may have, a fine table is not one of them. As Mr Armitage said, they have a monopoly and clearly prefer profit to people. I had thought that it would be good to sleep ashore again without the wretched pumping of the engines and smell of acrid smoke, but then I had not reckoned on swarms of voracious mosquitoes, packs of howling dogs, and cocks which strangely crowed from dusk till dawn. So I welcomed the dawn when finally it came and much looked forward to seeing the sites of the city. I breakfasted with Charlie and Mr Wallace, and Mr Wallace invited me to accompany them on a tour.

When we eventually emerged from the hotel we were met by a vast sea of people, each clutching the halter of a donkey with one hand and attempting to grab one of us with the other, and meanwhile shouting at the tops of their voices. The enthusiasm and loudness of Alexandrian donkey-boys cannot be exaggerated. Clearly they had no intention of seeking our opinion as to what we wished to do. After a rapid glance at the multitude, Mr Wallace told us to follow him and ventured forth waving his arms. I should here tell you that he is over six feet tall, but none the less I almost immediately lost sight of him as the crowd closed in, hands clutched at me and soon I found myself being bodily lifted up and swung astride a donkey. This at least got me into the open air again – and just in time to see Mr Wallace neatly captured. As he struggled between two beasts the man behind grasped their tails and held them together just as the man in front forced their heads together. And he was stuck. But with arms swinging he pushed on and suddenly the boy in front disappeared, whether felled by a blow or tripped I could not tell. But this opened an escape route to the side of the street where he grasped two beasts by their head bands and turned to look for us. The commotion had meanwhile distracted my own captor and I managed to dismount and push my way to Mr Wallace's side. From there we could see Charles sticking up above the maelstrom of men and beasts, evidently astride a donkey. Clearly our only way to rejoin him was to mount and this we did. Ah, and it was a choice sight to see the large Mr Wallace with feet almost touching the ground riding such a small ass through the streets of Alexandria, through crowds of Jews and Arabs, Turks and Greeks, and yelling donkey-boys. Charles and I, mindful of those pictures of Our Lord on his final entry to Jerusalem, rode like disciples behind. And laughed.

The town is like no town you have ever seen, Harry. The dusty streets are lined with square white houses, mostly two-storied with flat roofs and furnished with cool verandas shaded by lovely creepers. Amongst them are public squares, oases planted with trees and flowering shrubs. And thus, displayed as the captives of our proud donkey-boys, we three visited bazaars where stalls of exotic fruit and other foods were presided over by women entirely enveloped in great black shrouds, and mosques with tall minarets, and then a slave market where poor Mr Wallace was almost pulled to pieces for 'baksheesh', and finally the Pasha's new palace, the interior of which was gorgeous. Charles and I were greatly enjoying ourselves, safe upon our mounts, but I could almost hear the sigh of relief from Mr Wallace when our hotel finally hove in view. That evening, over a meal remarkably replete in meat of many descriptions, he enjoined us to read Thackeray's *First day in the East* which he said perfectly encapsulated our day's escapades. This I have still to do, but you, Harry, must do so if you can, so that you can more clearly see what your friend has suffered.

That evening we started our journey overland to Cairo and onwards to Suez on the Red Sea. On the Mahmoudieh Canal we embarked on a string of four barges, two for us and two for our luggage, all towed by the neatest little steam tug. This puffed eastwards overnight to a place called Atfeh on the Nile, where our little caravan entered a lock and was raised to river level. There, the steamer *Cairo* was waiting for us which, though horribly hot and crowded, provided us with a fascinating day's journey up this great highway. The country was perfectly flat and the banks, scattered with mud villages and palm trees, were green with irrigated crops. Everywhere people and their animals could be seen, camels carrying burdens, buffaloes turning water wheels. And the river too was crowded, endless boats with great triangular sails which moved rapidly out of our way as the *Cairo* belching smoke hove in sight.

As night fell the banks were lit by innumerable fires which no doubt allowed our vessel to find her passage in the darkness. There were only limited berths below and I with Charles and Jack chose happily to remain on deck with the bulk of the passengers. There we got little rest but spent the time in talking and gazing into the dark and playing noughts and crosses, and we were well pleased when, some time after midnight, the lights of Cairo appeared.

Again we were conducted efficiently to a hotel which proved to be surprisingly quiet, a blessing as that morning we were up at 6 o'clock for the next stage of our travels. After a splendid breakfast served to us by a waiter who, truly, rejoiced in the name Ali-baba, we set off in a caravan of small omnibuses on a remarkably well organised journey eastwards across the desert to Suez. The vehicles, mounted on two tall wheels, carried six passengers three abreast under a canvas roof. Although resembling both in appearance and comfort rather grand bathing machines, their open sides at least afforded a fine view of the passing scenery. Each was drawn by two mules in the shafts and two horses on ahead which were changed every 5 miles, and at every fourth stage, about 3 hours, the passengers were refreshed at dilapidated inns. I shared my machine with Charlie

*Ali-baba*

and Mr Wallace and three of the more cheerful cadets, and immediately behind was another which carried all five of the Armitages whose enthusiasms had lightened various moments of the voyage and who here did not disappoint, even when confronted by the wayside refreshments. The road was merely a cutting in the sand, lined throughout its length with the skeletons of countless camels; later when darkness fell it must have been with great difficulty that the drivers kept from straying off it into the desert itself. This was an undulating sea not of sand but of gravel and as parched as could be imagined, but as the day warmed, the distant hills appeared to be islands in an inland sea, the mirage of water being almost perfect. Early in the afternoon we passed the Indian and Australian mails going north, about 600 boxes as well as numerous parcels and heaps of passengers' baggage, all on an endless train of camels, some thousands in all.

It was an enjoyable but long day for we did not reach Suez until midnight, having covered almost a hundred miles. This proved a wretched little town and the hostelry provided was particularly unpleasant. There was virtually no water for washing and none for drinking, and for both we had an urgent need after a hundred miles of desert. Our thirst was somewhat quenched by tepid beer before we retired to attempt some sleep, disturbed as we were not only by mosquitoes but this time also by an army of insatiable fleas. So when dawn broke we rose with alacrity and made our way to the *Bengal* which was to carry us on the next stage of our journey. And so, on Saturday 25 March, 17 days out of Southampton, we set sail again down a narrow sea under the fiercest sun.

Somewhere in the Red Sea Jack Armitage died. Oh, it makes me so sad to recall him. How fragile we are and how tenuous our lives! 'He cometh up, and is cut down, like a flower'. On Sunday strong and lively and on Tuesday dead, wrapped in cloth with weighted feet, stretched on a board below the Union Jack. All who were free joined the family as the Captain read the burial service, and then the board was raised and the body plunged into the sea, the ripples of its falling soon lost in the ship's wash as we sped on our way. Thus went almost silently and for ever a son and brother, and a friend. But despite my tears, how glad I was to be there, embarked on this adventure, and not safe under cold grey skies.

And so we passed on down this desolate and narrow sea to Aden, a bleak place and hotter than anywhere I could have imagined. Not surprisingly few chose to go ashore, our lives instead being enlivened by visits from officers of the Naval frigates gathered there to stem the trade in slaves. For them, the regular arrival of P & O steamers with their company, their food and their drink is a much anticipated event. When coaling was complete we were again on our way, across the ocean towards India. The *Bengal* is a much more comfortable vessel than the *Euxine*, newer, only two years old, and more luxurious, her cabins larger and her passage smoother, screws being a fine improvement on paddles. And the season was a good one for our crossing for in the middle of the year the monsoon makes this passage rough. But our small circle was subdued. We all missed Jack, and the Armitages withdrew into themselves and the voyage now seemed a sad one. And I think it was sensing this that Mr Wallace introduced Charles and me to his book on the Malay language, the common tongue of the lands for which we were bound. And I found that not only did this distract me as intended but that in fact I have some capacity for memorising strange and unconnected words, and so have come to hope that in time I will master this form of speech.

At Galle in Ceylon, an earthly paradise after Suez and Aden, we again changed ships. The *Bengal* was bound for Calcutta and so we boarded the *Pottinger*, a paddler like the *Euxine* but even older and a great come-down after the comforts of the *Bengal*. I was sad to say goodbye to the Armitages; they remained distraught, and no longer relished their stay there as they had when buoyed by Jack's enthusiasms. And so we sailed on, celebrating Easter on the high seas, my spirits also being resurrected as the great ship throbbed its way eastwards. We were now some days behind schedule and so the stop at Penang was brief and we could do no more than view the town, a visit to the waterfalls and the hill taking too long. Here it was that I got my first sight of those communities in which I was to make my home, communities of all colours, languages and faiths, but my impressions I will leave until I tell you of Singapore. And so we continued south down the Straits, our last two days at sea. As the coasts of the peninsula and Sumatra crowded in upon us, so the calm waters contained ever greater numbers of boats of all descriptions, mostly small fishing vessels with brown mat sails but also larger trading vessels, some of the strangest shapes. Mr Wallace pointed out the old town of Malacca huddled on the shore with a decent mountain rising behind. And then through a maze of small islands as a thunderstorm struck to Singapore.

And so, Harry, this is where I came in. I have been here now more than a week and am getting acquainted with the place, and this I must start to describe to you when next I write. But I hope I have given you a little sense of the journey here, and, very much, that you will be able to follow in my wake, as it were, before too long. I trust that your parents are well. Please tell them that I am safe, and give my good wishes to Helen and Will.

From your well travelled friend,

*Ben*

*Penang from the Sea.*

*Wednesday, 3 May 1854*

My dear Harry,

Well, here I am again, less than a week since I posted my first letter to you, but I am longing to tell you more about this place. I have written to my family, but find it more difficult to tell them of my doings, and so I write to you again of our arrival and my first adventures.

As the *Pottinger* steamed into Singapore, winding between numerous small islands, the rain poured down, with thunder and lightening the like of which I had never seen before. But the storm cleared as quickly as it had come, and the sun was out as the town came into view. This lies along a crescent of shore in front of low tree-covered hills, the nearest, dominating the town, being Government Hill with the Governor's bungalow upon its crest. To the left lay a jumble of low roofs crowded together which later acquaintance showed to be the Chinese town on the west bank of the river, whilst to the right could be seen a long line of fine houses and bungalows with an open esplanade in front, the European town, and beyond these to the north, scattered wooden houses set amongst coconut trees above which the minaret of a mosque appeared.

The new harbour lies to the south of the settlement at Tanjong Pagar, and there lay HMS *Spartan*, her flag proudly announcing to whom the place belonged. No sooner had we dropped anchor than we were assailed by a flotilla of little boats loaded with goods of amazing variety: one crammed with wonderfully coloured fruits nearly all new to me, another with parrots of every hue with a few monkeys tethered amongst them, another filled to the brim with shellfish of all shapes and sizes. And then, less foreign to a man who knows the Thames, there were boats bringing fresh bread, eggs, milk, chickens and ducks, both alive and cooked, fish and vegetables, but here the boatmen are as varied, in looks and language, as the articles they have to sell. Although much was aimed at replenishing the ship, the passengers also threw themselves with enthusiasm into the bargaining, money or old clothes,

*Singapore from the Sea.*

handkerchiefs and hats, being exchanged for a great number of noisy animals and other useless objects.

Amongst the boats sailed a handful of tiny canoes formed from a single log, each with a dark skinned boy who shouted at us to throw coins into the water. Their black hair was bleached by the sun and sea, and as they paddled they bailed with a regular sweep of the hollowed foot. When a coin was tossed, with one movement they laid the paddle aside and dived in with hardly a splash, and then a few moments later one emerged holding the coin aloft, a huge smile splitting his brown face. 'Apa khabar?' I shouted, using my newly learnt Malay. 'Khabar baik' they shouted back, laughing and waving. And so I arrived in Singapore, England just six weeks behind us but a world away.

Soon we saw some lighters approaching and thus were conveyed to the shore. The date – Tuesday the 18th of April. There my uncle met me, and when my luggage had been gathered we set off on the short drive to the town. Here I must tell you a little about Uncle Tom with whom I am staying. He's a kindly fellow, somewhat short but with a cheerful face and ready smile, and, in contrast to most of my family, appears ready to listen to others, even those below him in status or in age. Arriving here about 15 years ago, he first worked for the people with whom he has found me employment, Martin, Dyce & Company, but was soon taken up as Superintendent of Police and Deputy Magistrate. So he is very much a pillar of our small establishment; indeed, as I write he is attending a meeting of the Masons, the lodge here active with over a hundred members. You can see that, thus uncled, I am in a favoured position.

I admit to finding myself unable to call Mrs Dunman 'Aunt Mary' as there is so little difference in our ages, so I address her as Mrs Dunman. She is truly from Singapore as both her grandfather and father settled here in the 1820s and her parents live here still. Indeed, the day we arrived Mary was at her parents' house as her mother was about to be delivered of another daughter! I will not bother you with the children of the house as I have hardly managed to name them yet. Suffice it to say that the eldest, Robert, is about 6 and the youngest but newly emerged. Mary is thin and dark, with the loveliest head of thick black hair and lively eyes, but she is very silent, I think from choice rather than that she has nothing worth saying, and devotes all her time to husband and children.

The Dunmans live on Beach Road, the road that runs north along the coast from the European quarter to the Malay village or 'kampong'. This is lined on one side by about 20 fine villas each set in its own garden or compound, 'bungalows' in the local parlance, the whole being "Twenty House Street" to the sensible Chinese. Their house, white walled and red tiled, is built around a central room which is windowless but with a lofty roof ventilated at the cone, and lighted from the surrounding rooms which are also spacious and open on to deep verandas. The windows have no glass but are covered with finely woven blinds or tatties to keep out the heat, and numerous punkahs also help to ventilate the place.

"Punkahs! What are punkahs? He's gone native already" I hear you cry. These excellent contraptions derived from India, a fabric covered wooden frame hanging from the ceiling which swings to and fro like a pendulum. A chord goes from the punkah around the ceiling and down to the hands of a boy, the punkah-wallah, or more often to his foot which he rhythmically moves. A dull job if ever there was one. My uncle says that one of his acquaintances, when his card parties go late into the night, shortens the chord and insists that his boy perches on a high stool which sounds a little unkind.

*Punkah*

The bedroom I have been given is very spacious and, if hardly cool, is not unbearably hot even at the height of the day. The floor is of red brick with fine woven matting, the walls painted white and decorated solely with chichaks, the nicest little lizards you can imagine, which entertainingly rush about uttering their name and keeping the insects in check. Attached is the bathroom containing little but a tiled floor drained in the middle and a huge water-pot. Europeans newly arrived have been known to try to climb into the pot to bathe, but I had already been warned against such ignorant behaviour. Rather, you stand beside the pot armed with a hand-bucket and dash cool water over your naked self. Very refreshing.

Now, Harry, you will not want to hear further about my bathing habits so let us turn to Singapore itself. The island, somewhat diamond shaped and about 25 miles from east to west and 14 from north to south, is separated from the Malay peninsular by straits less than a mile wide. The whole place is low and undulating, the highest hill, Bukit Timah or the Hill of Tin, being of only about 500 feet. From the town, which lies to the east of the southern point, two roads penetrate inland, one north-west to Bukit Timah and the other, the Serangoon road, north-eastwards.

I find it difficult to know where to start in describing the town, for although it is of no more than moderate size, what it lacks in scale it more than compensates for in interest. Here is a meeting of all mankind – all colours and sizes, all voices and beliefs. Here are brown Malays along the beach, their sarongs, a simple sheath of patterned cloth, rolled above their knees as they empty their boats of crabs and fish and shells. Klings from the Coromandel coast as dark as their shops, their women in their brilliant saris splashing the streets with colour. Parsees and Bengalis white robed with curious hats, Jews dressed like Moses, clerks of indeterminate race from Malacca, Bengali grooms, sailors from Java and all the islands of the Archipelago. And everywhere the Chinese, from the towkay, richer than any European, to the farmer in his field, every inch carpeted with crops, to the teaming bazaars, the wharves by the river and the boats themselves. And amongst all this we Europeans stride, tall and pink and perspiring.

But all this mix is not jumbled together but neatly arranged as Raffles planned. When you join me here (and I say 'when') we will walk through the town from the north, starting in the village of Bugis people by the Rochor River, great seafarers and traders, then passing to Kampong Glam with its mosque for the Malays and raised houses of wood thatched with leaves, then through the Arab and Indian quarter and past the elegant houses of the Europeans to the Plain by St Andrew's Church. Then crossing the river we will come to the bustles and smells of the Chinese town, dense and hectic, and wend our way through the crowds towards the beach.

And here is the harbour which fully echoes the bustle and colour of the town. It is crowded with vessels of every conceivable sort; with elegant men-of-war and trading vessels from Europe, steam vessels belonging to the Company and the P & O, Chinese junks with their arched sides painted in curving streaks of red, yellow and white, Siamese ships, half European in style but with huge carved stems, these lying next to the long, low prahus from the archipelago, as graceful as slender fish. And busy amongst them are lighters and small rowing boats ferrying goods and people between the go-downs by the river and the seagoing vessels. And in the distance beyond, belching smoke, sails the *Java* on her way to Batavia with the mail from Holland, a journey of three or four days.

I am told that if we kept our ears open on such a walk we should be able to hear from Europe

*Chichak*

26

Street Scene

Dutch, German, Spanish and Portuguese as well as English, then a multitude of forms of Chinese and Indian, and of course Malay which is the *lingua franca* of the place. In all, 17 different languages and 15 different dialects!

Here I am filling pages with description but telling you little of what I have been doing which I now fear will have to wait until my next letter. But let me at least follow up the fate of my travelling companions, the naturalist Mr Wallace and his assistant Charlie Allen. They have now gone into the interior to start their work and I hope to be able to visit them there before too long. However I did see a little of them before they left and Mr Wallace kindly invited me to dinner at the London Hotel where they were lodged. This is the larger of the two hostelries in town and nicely situated on the Esplanade, but is said to be even less hospitable than the Hotel de Paris. The proprietor is a Mr Dutronquoy, a Frenchman from Jersey, so both establishments have connections to that land where the skills of mine host are so ably displayed, but these have sadly not proved translatable to a tropical setting. Certainly, the meal we had together there did not do justice to the company, the food looking as unappetising as it tasted, and the waiter as unappetising as the food – warm, damp and ill-presented. As the place has been made from two fine houses joined together, inside it is a warren of rooms and passages, and Charlie told me that their bedrooms were almost as unattractive as the meal, ill-furnished, far from the bathroom, and anyway placed over a late-night bar and bowling alley. And all for five dollars a night! No wonder Mr Wallace spoke with such enthusiasm about starting his work in the forest.

But I should say that Mr Dutronquoy has another claim to fame here; ten years ago he became the Settlement's first daguerreotype artist. So if you should think this place far distant, still it is not lacking in access to the latest inventions. I myself will eschew such modern contrivances and continue with my sketching, the results of which I will no doubt send you from time to time for your edification.

Now, Harry, let me finish by assuring you that the food I have enjoyed here has generally been excellent in both quality and, more importantly for you, quantity. You will, I know, find both it and the place quite suited to your palate so I beg you to still consider joining me.

Hoping that you are as contented as your well fed friend,

*Ben*

Boat Quay.

*Thursday, 25 May 1854*

Dear Harry,

My plans to continue calmly describing this place to you are destroyed. We've had a riot! But I hasten to add that we are well; indeed, no European has been hurt, only the Chinese being harmed. The problem started on Friday three weeks ago when apparently there was in the market an altercation between a couple of Chinamen over the price of some bananas. Unfortunately, these men were originally from different parts of China, and therein lay the problem. Although we may think of all from that vast county as 'Chinese', yet they are highly clannish. Thus what started out as an argument between Hokkien and Teochew soon developed into blows, bystanders joined in, reinforcements were called, and soon whole streets were engulfed. My uncle was of course quickly involved, and within an hour or two he assessed the situation as serious and went post-haste to the Governor. Our Governor, of whom I must tell you more anon, holds firmly to the belief that the sight of the chief representative of the Honourable Company will calm any situation, and he rode forth on his horse, only to be pelted by the mob and forced to rapidly retire. By then all of us had hurried home from our offices, and as darkness fell we could see the glows of fires burning in the Chinese town. Uncle was home very late and away before dawn, leaving instructions that we were to stay in the house and that I should take care of Mrs Dunman and the children.

The next day rioting continued in the town. Police successfully cleared the streets but as soon as they moved on trouble started again. By the Sunday the rioters found that streets restricted their violence and so moved into the country where a number of pitched battles were fought. This caused me to worry about how my naturalist friends from the ship were faring, for Bukit Timah where they are has a Chinese population of some hundreds. But my uncle assured me that the violence remained only Chinese against Chinese and he felt by this time confident that Europeans were largely safe.

Certainly, the streets around Beach Road were quite undisturbed, and Mrs Dunman and the children remained calm although confined to house and garden. Worse were the poor Chinese servants who could neither return home nor learn the fate of their families.

On the Monday, all was quiet and I went down to the river with some other lads. Here it was peaceful, with the boat dwellers seemingly going about their business as usual. But there were rumours of terrible violence in the country, so the crews of three Naval ships now with us, the *Sybille, Lily* and *Rapid*, were called upon to assist, and various residents and ships' officers were sworn in as Special Constables. By Wednesday calm had returned to the town but no shop dared yet to open as the countryside was still in turmoil, with plantations attacked and gangs parading around with heads carried aloft on spears. So the Company's steamer *Hooghly* set forth around the island to land parties of troops at strategic points. On Thursday the first shops opened their shutters and the servants ventured out to see what they could find to buy. Not until Sunday the 14th did all return to normal. Thus after a week of enforced idleness I returned to work on the Monday.

And that was the day your letter arrived, together with one from my father my first from England. I am so glad to hear from you and to get news of your doings and of family and friends. Yes, I envy you the party with sweet Harriet but little else besides. Is Will still struck on her? And no surprise to hear that Bradshaw remains his ugly self. Our office here contains none like him, the Lord be praised.

And yes, I am already making enquiries about employment here that may suit you. I understand how your parents are loath to let you launch forth to distant lands without the prospect of a secure livelihood, and I value the trust they put in my judgement of the place's suitability for their youngest son. And yet, with a little help from your oldest friend, I am confident that you will persuade them.

Despite the excitement of riots, and the strain put upon police and troops, yesterday the Queen's birthday was duly marked. It is a fact that in celebrating the Queen attaining 35 years of age we also celebrate the same for this Settlement for both were born in the same year. A ball was thought inappropriate under the circumstances, but another event had long been planned. In the calm of the morning, the Governor and other dignitaries including my uncle and aunt repaired to an island about 15 miles south-west of the town there to lay the foundation stone of a lighthouse. One has long been clamoured for at this place, and it will be named in honour of the Settlement's founder. Raffles remains much revered here.

Now it is time that I tell you a little about the native peoples who are, of course, the real essence of the place. The month I have been here is far too short a time to get their measure, but my uncle is a fount of knowledge and ever willing to enlighten his ignorant nephew. From the rioting I have at least learned something of the Chinese, and by good fortune I already have one whom I can call a friend. Lim Wee Cheng is a fellow clerk in Martin, Dyce and Company where he sits all day reading and writing letters, translating from Malay to English to Chinese with great skill and even greater patience. He is not much older than I, shorter with a flat face and broad nose on which his large glasses perch precariously so that he is always pushing them back into place. He laughs readily over the merest trifle, his narrow eyes shutting so that I must be careful not to joke with him when walking in the street or he will walk straight into posts or people. His father came here from Malacca and so sent his son back to the College there for his education; Chinamen seem to value education in a way our fellow-countrymen seem not to do. So Lim speaks a fine local English and this, with his ambition, will see him go far. Being Chinese he calls me 'Pen', a most suitable name for a clerk, and he has taken upon himself the task of educating Pen in Chinese ways.

Ah, the name 'Lim Wee Cheng' – let me explain. Chinamen have three names each. He is 'Mr Lim', 'Wee Cheng' being 'Harry' but seldom used except within the family. All his brothers may be Wee too, but different Wees. All most logical and sensible.

Certainly the Chinese dominate everywhere, the harbour, the town and even the countryside. It is said that the population of the island now numbers some 70,000 souls of which about half are Chinamen. Then come the Malays, the true natives, and then the Klings and others from India. Of Europeans there are estimated to be about 400, the majority from our own dear country. Now add to that a kaleidoscope of Arabs, Jews, Parsees, Armenians, Cochin-Chinese, Javanese, Siamese and half-castes, and the babel of a dozen languages and you may get a flavour of the place.

Although it is rumoured that the Chinese knew of the island many centuries ago, it is only since the English came that they have settled here in numbers. My uncle tells me that last year alone brought 12,000 newcomers. Most hail straight from the home land, but over the years a number have come, like Lim's father, from the other Settlements as our wealth outgrew that of Malacca and Penang. Many have mothers who are Malay but they remain Chinese to the core. And many speak English very well, particularly those educated at Malacca College, and these, such as Lim, are much valued as clerks.

Those who come directly from China are mostly poor and very largely men, the 'sinkehs' from the south of their country, leaving poverty with the dream of making their fortunes in the Southern Seas and so returning home. They arrive by the boat-load, some no more than children, and I have stood by the beach as they land, herded ashore by the broker who has paid their passage and will arrange their bondage. For the healthy a bond will cost the purchaser perhaps 50 dollars for the year, but the sickly can be had for much less. Some go off to wealthy homes, for Europeans particularly favour Chinese as servants as they are ever diligent, seeking not just to pay off the bond but to save as well so that they can remit money back to those they have left behind. But most, with their meagre possessions, are led off to a coolie house where they will lodge.

These houses are run by what are called 'kongsi', a sort of friendly society for people from one clan or village or occupation. Some of the English seem most suspicious of the kongsi, seeing them as little different from the secret societies that foment crime and other troubles, but Lim tells me that this is not so. Rather, they act in lieu of family and there the sinkehs will be looked after, finding a home, friends, a job, help in times of trouble, and if the worst occurs, a decent burial.

The men are quite short, flat of face and pale of skin. Universally, they shave the head in front and tie the hair remaining in a long pigtail hanging down behind. When about their work both rich and poor dress most sensibly in loose shirt and trousers. In the early days nearly all were unmarried as women seldom accompanied them from their land, though some took Malays as their wives. But more recently whole families have been arriving, and it is said that now perhaps a quarter of the Chinese are women. Although seldom seen on the streets, they may be glimpsed at temples or in the far recesses of a house, darkly dressed in wide trousers and short jacket buttoned to the throat, their hair drawn back tightly to a bun behind, and carrying on a hip a plump baby, its face thickly powdered as if prepared for cooking.

And speaking of cooking ["Ah ha" I hear you murmur, "I knew he would soon get on to food"], last week we had a most interesting, if Christian, dinner at our house for some, if not of the Great, at least of the Good. The guests were our missionaries, the Keasburys, Miss Cooke and Mr Song. I gathered that the Dunmans had for long meant to do such entertaining, and my coming had finally galvanised them, hoping to christianise their wayward nephew.

Miss Cooke, not even the most distant of relatives I hasten to add, must be about 30, quite severe and loud as befits a missionary. She came here only a year ago to take over and revitalise the small Christian school for Chinese girls. This she has now successfully accomplished, and we can be confident that her pupils will be well disciplined to counteract the enervating climate and materialism which she believes are the curses of Singapore.

Mr Benjamin Keasbury, who has of course a splendid first name, has an equally delightful middle name – Peach, which he certainly does not resemble. He is a small man, well into middle age, with a serious air, and is I know much respected in the community by all races and classes. Certainly, he is a mine of information and a fount of surprisingly good stories. In his younger days he travelled much, from his home in India to Singapore and Batavia as a merchant and then to America. There, gaining a wife and a religion, he returned here some 15 years ago as a missionary and has never since left the place. Now, helped by an able if quiet wife, he ministers in a chapel with an enthusiastic congregation of Chinese and Malays, runs a school for boys, translates the gospels and manages his own Mission

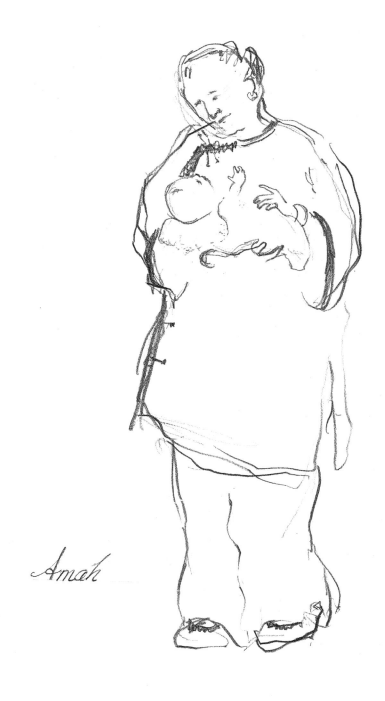

Amah

Press, has created a small fruit and spice plantation on the edge of town, and is a friend of both the Governor and the poor. And Miss Cooke worries about enervation!

But the most surprising guest was Mr Song Hoot Kiam, not that he was Chinese for those other than Europeans are often entertained here, but that he was educated in Scotland! Although an earnest Christian he is a most pleasant dinner companion, and not much older than I. He told me that he was born in Malacca and came to the attention there of a Scotsman, Dr Legge, who took him and two others to school in a place called Huntly in the north-east of that country. Although they must have been the only Chinese for many, many miles he says he was well treated and so turned to the native religion, being soon baptised a Christian. It was most interesting to hear of his impressions of a place so far from his own. As I find here conducive to me, so he found Scotland, the warmth of the people compensating for the chill of the climate. Finishing his schooling in two years he briefly toured England, this amazingly including an audience with the Queen and Prince Albert! Then, returning to Malacca, he heard upon reaching Singapore of suitable employment and so never completed his journey.

A dinner in a European's house such as ours gives me a particular delight – no, not just in the food but in the mix. The Malay amah comes to take the children to bed, the Indian butler enters to serve the drinks, and then we go through to the dining room. There the table is set as in England with silver, with cushioned chairs, the pictures on the wall and the measured calm as fine as any English home. And what has the Chinese cook prepared for our delectation? Indian mutton with Java potatoes and Malacca vegetables may be reminiscent of home, but then there are the spicy soups, the hot sambals, the rich curries, the salted turtles eggs, followed by tapioca puddings of all shapes and sizes, and then fruit, and all washed down with pale ale. You, glutton that you are, will love it.

It is this mix, this variety in the place, that so appeals to me. Take the clothing that everywhere surrounds us. The people are ablaze with colour, clothes of all forms and hues drifting or hurrying through the streets. Of course the local people, whether Malays, Chinese or Kling, know exactly how to dress in such a climate, all cool and loose-fitting. Only the Englishman, with his tight jacket, waistcoat and trousers and horrible hat and cravat, exhibits mere manners and no sense.

And so, exhibiting both sense and manners as befits a friend of yours, I must close and hurry off to work. Take every good care of yourself and your family.

Your friend the clerk,

*Jen*

Betel Palm

*Thursday, 15 June 1854*

Dear Harry,

Greetings again from your tropical friend. I remain well and am finding that, to date, this place seems to suit me most admirably. Now I have been here almost two months and have still told you nothing of the people other than the Chinese. Certainly it is the Chinaman, his life and looks and language, whom I find of greatest fascination but the others have their fascinations too.

The Malays are a very different people from the Chinese. Dark of skin with waving hair, they are seafarers and farmers, all Mohammedans. Within the town they live mostly at Kampong Glam to the north, although another 'kampong' or village is now being built to the south. Kampong Glam is certainly the most relaxed and peaceful of communities, the houses widely scattered, mostly of wood and raised on stilts, with large eaves over cool balconies overlooking shady gardens. Here a multitude of fruit trees grow, bananas with their huge leaves, mango trees with hanging yellow fruits, the tall and graceful betel palm. Down by the Rochor River the houses are built out over the water, boats tied below and gardens stretching behind. From my travels elsewhere on the island this seems a preference for the Malays are indeed an aquatic people.

Of a morning, the men can be seen sitting by their doors, chewing betel nuts, with their sarongs, which usually hang loosely from the waist, wrapped around to shelter them from the cool morning breeze. From the back of the house smoke is rising as the women prepare the first meal of the day. And then all foregather on the veranda to eat, grandparents, parents and a host of children sitting around a mat on which is spread a fine collection of dishes.

Here amongst the Malays can be seen more family life than in the rest of the town put together. Of course women, so rare amongst the immigrants, abound here and so children abound. And then much of their life is spent outside in this warm climate. The women are small and neat, their long dark hair tied behind, their clothes at home simply a sarong tied above the breasts, a loose shirt added when they venture from the village. Men also use only the sarong at home but add trousers and shirt when going out, with a red handkerchief tied rakishly around the head. The children are mostly naked, wonderfully brown with mops of black hair and great dark eyes. You know the expression 'his face lit up'? Well, you will know its truth when one of these children looks up at you and smiles.

Our third group, the Klings, come from all parts of India, but mainly from the south, the Coromandel coast, and not all of them voluntarily. From early days convicts have been sent here, initially to the horror of the locals, but in fact they have proved most valuable in a place where labour is both scarce and expensive. Sensibly, the Engineer in charge of public works also doubles as the Superintendent of Convicts, and so many of the roads and bridges, and of the finest buildings, have been built by them. They also are favoured as servants. For all these labours they are paid, and when their time is done many have stayed on as owners of cattle or of horses for hire, as brick-makers, carpenters or blacksmiths, or in service. It is the Klings who provide the grooms and syces for the rich, and also all the washermen, though why there is this division of labour I am unsure.

On the outskirts of the town lies Dhoby Ghaut, a most unlikely place, a large field filled with washermen. There by the river may be seen dozens of Klings, both men and women, busily beating clean all manner of garments. They do not favour scrubbing clothes, but rather enthusiastically beating them upon rocks, rinsing and beating again. All types of laundry are treated thus, from hardy trousers to the most delicate of shifts, and from all parts of society. And then they are hung to dry, a most varied and colourful array, gentlemen's jackets and servants' shirts in much closer proximity than would ever be allowed when worn.

Most Klings are Hindus but some are Mohammedans like the Malays, and there are temples and mosques especially for them. Whereas the Chinese and Malay quarters can readily be identified, Klings who are much fewer in number are more widely scattered. Their merchants and traders are found south of the river with the Chinese, served by both temples and mosques fitted in amongst the houses. Here they set up shop selling particularly cloth, the interiors dark with hangings of the richest colours, but spoiled for viewing by the loud persistence of the salesmen. The Chinese are more subtle in their persuasions.

If the men are unattractive, dark and stringy, their women, even the wives of the poorest, are often of a colour and elegance unsurpassed by other races. Imagine a woman, tall and thin, striding on bare feet coolly through the steaming streets, one elegant arm supporting a pitcher of water on her head. Her long black hair is gathered in a bun, her body draped in yards of cotton of wonderful colours but with a shoulder bare, her dark brown skin set off by gold ornaments on wrist and ankle, with rings on her fingers, her ears and, yes, even through one nostril. How would Harriet like thus to be adorned?

But look, there is a carriage stopping down the street! The groom runs round to open the door and a European lady alights, her pale face already moist with perspiration, her waist pinched in, her skirts voluminous as she totters on high heels to the nearest shop, appareled unsuitably for this or indeed any other climate. The master race? Ha!

The Master of this master race is our Governor and, having now had the honour of calling upon him in company with Uncle Tom, it is time that I tell you something of the Honourable Colonel William George Butterworth, commonly called Butterpot the Great. The comments I hear about him are, shall I say, varied, some muttering 'the kindest and most hospitable of men', others 'a compound of ignorance and pomposity'. Obviously my acquaintance is of the slightest, and unlikely to get more intimate, but I would hazard that both comments have some truth. Meeting me, he was both kind and considerate although I personally was of no consequence. Certainly, this may have been my uncle's doing, for the Governor greatly respects him, and rightly so, but then he was more attentive than duty demanded. But on the other hand, he rides around the town in a large and specially built carriage with four in hand and from this will recognise only those of suitable eminence, and he certainly seems inordinately fond of sumptuous engineering works, each edifice bearing a metal plaque with his name prominent upon it.

But saying that, Government House is in fact surprisingly modest, sitting on the hill which overlooks the town. The old name of the place was Bukit Larangan or the Forbidden Hill, and I suppose it still is to the natives with Butterpot on the summit, but to the Europeans it is simply The Hill. Raffles chose the site, and indeed the present house is still in part his original dwelling. It is a wooden bungalow partly thatched like native houses, consisting of two parallel halls with front and back verandas terminated by two square wings which comprise the sleeping quarters. The view from the front veranda is very fine, overlooking the European town with its white walled, red roofed houses scattered amongst a sea of green, and so to the harbour studded with countless ships.

The Settlement over which Butterpot rules revolves solely around Commerce, and Commerce is centered on the river which is in consequence the heart of the place, alive by day and night. From the anchorage the river mouth is completely hidden, but as you approach the shore and swing left around the Fort, the view changes dramatically for the river, so narrow at its mouth, suddenly expands into a fine basin sweeping round on the western side until it closes again, a quarter of a mile up, to be as narrow as the entrance.

On the right, England and the Honourable Company are triumphant. To emphasise their masterly role stands the Dalhousie Obelisk commemorating the Governor-General's visit a few years ago, a proud erection. Then, by a fine grove of angsana trees, comes the Police Office where my uncle works, then Post Office and Court House which backs on to the splendid offices of the Governor. Two English ship-yards then interpose themselves, apparently to the discomfort of the lawyers, but both

Government Offices

Commercial Square

Dalhousie Obelisk

have been there many years and are successful. One, and you would see what I mean by 'English' if you could read their large sign "Messrs Wilkinson, Tivendale & Co.", has been building steamers now for six years, their first, the little *Ranee,* often busy around the harbour.

To the left Commerce reigns supreme. Fine warehouses or 'go-downs' line Boat Quay, the ground floor for merchandise and the first for merchants and their clerks. Those nearer the mouth belong to Europeans, and here it is that I spend my days, whilst those of the Chinese further up the river are both more substantial and more colourful, the balconies hung with red banners. Ahead, where the river narrows, lies an iron bridge flanked by more go-downs, and above it Government House on its little hill.

The bridge, the first and busiest of the two which span the river, is one of my favourite places. Not only is the traffic over it of constant interest and variety, but it provides the finest view of the basin itself. This is crowded with a multitude of boats, lighters or tongkangs carrying goods and smaller boats, sampans, with human cargoes. But most, in fact, are not scurrying about but tied to stakes and are the homes of countless families. Some are no more than 15 by 4 feet but, with a tiny canvas shelter across the middle, harbour father, mother, children, ducks, rabbits and a pig. The smallest children have a string tied round their middles so that if they fall overboard someone can haul them in, that is assuming they're still attached to the other end. Although from the smell of the place, as noisome as our own sweet Thames, you might think that a ducking would kill them anyway.

If I leave the bridge and go down to the quay, I will be assailed by boats for hire. "Two-man boat, sar?", "Four-man boat, sar?", "Pull like the debbel, sar!" And I could have a nice sampan pulled all day by a couple of powerful Malays for only 60 cents. But having written 'pulled' I mean 'pushed', for rowers here face forwards and not backwards as at home. Even the lighters, the tongkangs, are pushed, a number of men working one hefty oar.

Behind Boat Quay runs a road which curves parallel to it, ending at Fort Fullerton on Battery Point. At the gate two Sepoy sentries stand in the glare of the sun, in their red coats looking as if at any moment they might ignite. The Fort is now being rebuilt under the supervision of Captain Collyer of the Royal Engineers whom I have met at my uncle's. It will be three times its former glory, with new 56- and 68-pounders, a nice house for the officers in the centre, new barracks for the lower ranks, and all landscaped with handsome trees and shrubs.

I hear that most of the merchants think all this a great waste of money. But nearby in Commercial Square I can see that they themselves are not averse to a little grandeur. Here, a central garden with flowers and trees enclosed by a wooden railing is surrounded by fine buildings which house various shops and offices belonging to the Europeans. These include our new emporium, John Little & Co, and, best of all, the offices of the *Straits Times* which is one, and the newest, of our two papers and here has a splendidly large reading room to which anyone can repair to peruse a fine collection of newspapers

Boat Quay

*Hibiscus*

from both England and India. And we even have a public library, so if you come you should not fear that your intellect will wither in the tropical heat. And for your riches we have both the Union Bank of Calcutta *and* the Oriental Bank!

Now, Harry, I have been remiss in not telling you of the financial situation of your friend, for you will, I am sure, be eager to know how rich I am in this far outpost. Well, first about the currency. Here we are paid in dollars, worth five shillings, and not the Company rupee, worth two. Although a change to the rupee has been mooted, the idea causes consternation. If at dinner you want to cause apoplexy amongst the distinguished guests, ask in all innocence how soon the rupee will be introduced.

It is true that costs here are generally high, though I have more than once been surprised to see goods made in England sold more cheaply than in London. But the wages are certainly good, and you will be pleasantly surprised when I say that I earn the princely sum of 80 dollars each month, three times what I was paid in London. Sadly it leaves as fast as it arrives although, as you know I lead a most virtuous life, little of it is spent on vice. I hear rumoured that a man in my uncle's position would earn perhaps 400 dollars a month, so with servants at 5, the same as at home, people here can afford to live in some style.

Certainly, servants are plentiful. In one house I have visited there were a dozen: butler, under-servants, maid, cooks, grooms, gardeners, a washerman, scavenger and waterman (there is as yet no public water supply). And my uncle, although hardly the most affluent of men, has six which must be three times as many as he would have at home. There is his 'boy', although Tan must be in his late twenties, and my aunt's 'ayah' or maid. Then there is the cook, a water-carrier, a groom and a gardener.

Of course everyone complains of the cost of living, saying that if at home £500 suffices at least a thousand a year is needed here, but in truth this need is merely the desire to live at a level to which they would never aspire in England.

Since last I wrote I have, amongst many uplifting events, had one devastating encounter! Some weeks ago I met a man little older than I who not only is good-looking, as many Eurasians are, and always dressed most handsomely, but whose name is Tertullian de Souza! How can poor Benjamin Cook compete? He and his brother Manuel work for a neighbouring company, Aitken de Souza, so I am frequently reminded of my failings.

On this sad note I must leave you.
Your friend in warm places,

*Ben*

*Post script.* I enclose a sketch map of the town which I have copied out as it will help you better to follow my wanderings.

Buket Timah Forest

*Friday, 14 July 1854*

My dear Harry,

A month has flown since last I sent off a letter to you and it is high time that I tell you more of my doings. You will remember that I spoke of the naturalist Mr Wallace and his assistant Charlie Allen who came out to Singapore at the same time as I. Well, I have now visited them at their work in the forest. They are living in the centre of the island at Bukit Timah, the highest hill we have, if only of 500 feet. It lies about 8 miles from the town along a perfectly good road. On Friday last I arranged for a gharry to pick me up after lunch from my office, firstly to convey me home to collect some baggage and then take me to the forest.

Beyond Dhoby Ghaut houses are left behind and plantations start, acres of nutmegs and pepper and gambier. The estates belong to both Europeans and Chinese, some of whom live in the town, others in fine houses amongst their trees. The gharry goes at a good pace, the driver running beside the little ponies, and below the awning I enjoy the breeze from our passage. Soon the plantations give way to forest, forest very different from the woodlands of England. Most obviously, many of the trees are of immense size, the trunks huge and branching only at the greatest height.

We reached Bukit Timah in the late afternoon, a Chinese settlement of some size surrounding a Roman Catholic mission. Charlie was there, busily engaged in sorting the bugs he had collected that day, but Mr Wallace was still in the woods. Charlie was certainly happy to see me, confiding that the work was sometimes, and the evenings always, dull. He showed me to the house where he was staying, one attached to the mission, and it was there that I was given a bed. Mr Wallace soon returned, in great spirits over his afternoon's captures and pleased to see me, confiding later that Charles needed some young company. And so we went across for dinner with the missionary, who is French, omelet and vegetables as it was Friday.

The next day I accompanied Charlie to the forest. After he had prepared for the day's work, we breakfasted and then set forth at about 9 o'clock loaded with guns, nets and sundry bags. Mr Wallace is particularly keen on insects and amongst these on beetles. Now, Harry, do not laugh! Whereas in London you may think all beetles small, similar and dull, here they are as varied as can be imagined and often of remarkable shape and beautiful colour. Well worthy of an earnest collector as Mr Wallace proved when later he showed me his collection. But Charlie is not yet too enamoured of beetles, finding it much more exciting to shoot birds or mammals than peer under leaves or below logs for bugs.

As I have said, the forest here is very different from the woodlands at home. Yes, the trees are huge, but they are also, so I learned, very varied, so we do not have 'an oak wood' or 'a beech wood' but rather trees of endless variety. Amongst these we walked quite easily as Chinese wood-cutters had left many paths. As we went we collected any bugs we came across, which Charlie stored in various containers. Occasionally he would try to shoot something, but of mammals we saw none and of birds he obtained only two bedraggled specimens. Already he knew the paths quite well so there was no danger of being lost, and in fact we were seldom out of the hearing of the wood-cutters. By the middle of the afternoon we returned to the mission, Charlie to sort the creatures we had taken, I to wring out my shirt, for these forests are extremely hot, and then take a gentle nap.

On Sunday we attended the service in the church, St Joseph's, newly built by Father Maudit, a little man bustling and cheerful in manner. The place was well filled and the crowd enthusiastic, a nice contrast to the English church in town, the Chinese settled thereabouts almost all having converted to Christianity. And to my surprise, Harry, I was much moved by it all: the strange crowd, the Catholic rituals, the exuberant singing, and all in a voice of which I understood not a word yet praising the same God that we praise at home. After lunch it was in an elevated state that I returned to the town by the means I had come, most pleased to have glimpsed the island's interior.

Now, in case you think my time here is spent solely on pleasure interspersed with the occasional riot, I should tell you about my more usual life. There is no need to explain to you about my work, as clerking for a trading company is no mystery to either of us. Instead let me tell you about my typical working day and my typical repasts for I know that food is ever of interest to you. And to me.

For Europeans, the day starts at 5 am with the firing of the 68-pounder on The Hill. By half past the hour it is daylight and, after some coffee and toast, I venture out to join the community who are taking their exercise in the cool of the morning. European men can be seen walking or riding but never accompanied by their ladies. Many of the Chinese are already at work, coolies arriving from the interior laden with baskets of fresh produce, shopkeepers standing in their doorways talking loudly and enjoying some tobacco. The Malays are also astir in their kampong, smoke rising from the cooking fires and the children dashing hither and yon, naked in the cool air.

Fern frond

Butterfly

Beetle

Pitcher plant

Chinese Trader

Betel Nut Set

Then back home and a change into loose pyjamas or sarong for an hour or so with pen and paper or my sketchbook; reading at this time only sends me back to sleep. At 8 o'clock there might come a tap on the door, and there will be the itinerant Kling barber ready to shave me or cut my hair, services I seldom require. And then a cool bath and dressing for the business day, white trousers and a black jacket being the orthodox attire. Breakfast is served at 9 o'clock and if I have not been delayed by the barber, I will sit on the veranda waiting for the gong, and watch the world go by along Beach Road. Already, various traders are out, moving from house to house with their goods which are of great variety – fans, slippers, lacquer-ware and carved ivory from China, smoking caps, shawls and sarongs from India, and even socks and handkerchiefs from Europe. These are first offered at much the same price as would be found in London, but this allows the bargaining so deeply satisfying to both parties.

At last the gong sounds and we go in to breakfast, which is when we first see the ladies and children of the house. Of children the Dunmans have five, the eldest coming on for seven years old and the youngest for one, both boys with three girls between. They seem perfectly pleasant but with an attentive mother and servants are seldom seen, which I do not regret. The food set before us is both varied and abundant, a little fish, some curries and rice, eggs and bacon, followed by some wonderfully light bread with fresh butter, then plenty of fresh fruit, all washed down with tea, though Uncle sometimes prefers a glass of claret or beer. Breakfast over, the real business of the day commences. The carriage arrives to drive the men to town through busy streets. The first stop is Commercial Square, where news is gathered, but by 10 o'clock I have started work and toil away until lunch, or tiffin, at 1. The food is much the same as at breakfast though served cold, and, as the paper comes out at this time, half an hour's extra relaxation is taken to peruse and comment upon it. At 2 o'clock business is again under way but by half past 4 or so the day's work is done. Meanwhile the women seem to lead quiet lives in the coolness of their bungalows, waiting for callers before lunch, the usual time to leave your card, and perhaps venturing out to the shops and markets in the afternoon. Their greatest excitement seems to be the mail, and when ships are due to arrive or depart many more can be seen scurrying about the streets.

After work many, particularly the wealthy, repair to the Esplanade to take the air, and then may be seen much of the beauty and talent of the place, not only European but native too. Most simply walk or ride, frequently stopping to gossip, but the younger men may resort to the cricket ground or near-by fives courts. Fives, though rare at home, is of long standing here and very popular despite the heat; I am soon going to take it up. The crowds are greatest on Tuesday and Friday evenings for these are band evenings. Then the chains opposite Coleman Street are taken down and carriages and horsemen, usually forbidden on the Plain itself, mingle with those on foot around the band-stand to listen to the current regimental band for an hour or so. At present, I must say we have a very good band in residence, that of the 38th Regiment, and they play both at the Esplanade and on Wednesdays at the Sepoy Lines. By half past six it is all but dark and, as the oil lamps are lit along the streets, the crowds disperse. Across the Plain the hotel, now illuminated, is busy with those as yet unwilling to return to family duties, whilst those still unattached may linger by Scandal Point. This place, an old gun emplacement opposite St Andrews, is called thus not from the nakedness of the local boys who can be found swimming there at each high tide, but rather because all manner of people find it a favourite spot for rest and gossip, or to meet a special friend, both by day and night.

Except on band nights most retire home by 6 o'clock, there to enjoy a glass of sherry before dressing for dinner which is usually served at 6.30. This is again a decent meal; soup and fish are followed by beef or chicken served with potatoes and a fine variety of vegetables, all washed down with liberal quantities of beer. Then comes curry and rice accompanied by all kinds of sambals or native pickles, to be followed by pudding and sometimes by cheese and then a wonderful array of fruit, the centrepiece perhaps a pineapple surrounded by bananas, mangoes, rambutan, pomeloes and mangosteens. After the ladies retire, a cigar and a glass or two of sherry and the dinner is done. There is no doubt that the older residents are of the firm opinion that large dinners well washed down are necessary for sound health and a long life. And who am I to disagree with their wisdom. Then with a couple of hours before bed at 10 o'clock, a chat on the veranda or perhaps a book passes the hours pleasantly enough.

So you can see, my friend, that life in Singapore is not too onerous. And remember that always the days are warm, the sun is often beaming down, and the air, without the fires and fogs of London, is wonderfully clean and healthy. So surely you must be tempted to swap those cold grey days and that thick and noisome air for a place so fresh and warm and colourful? Am I tempting you?

And here I must tell you that I am making some progress with finding a post that will suit you. It appears that the trading houses are often short staffed as business is now growing so quickly, so any bright young fellow who arrives is assured of a good position. So I much look forward to your next letter when I hope you will confirm your intentions. Then I or my uncle can see what can be arranged.

Before I close I must tell you how things have worked out about our riot of two months ago. It was true that the violence was solely with the Chinese for not a single European was hurt nor any European property damaged, but it is said that over 400 Chinese were killed, many wounded and over 300 houses burnt, by far the greatest trouble that the settlement has ever experienced. And all for the sake of bananas! A total of about 500 people were arrested of which half were soon released and the others brought swiftly to trial. For much of June the talk was all of this trial, until finally on the 23rd the proceedings were rapidly wound up, with the great majority released for lack of evidence, 78

Pineapple

Durian

Mangosteens

Rambutan

sentenced to prison and only six to death. Early this month two were executed and the other four reprieved. Certainly, this whole episode, while dreadful for the great majority of the Chinese, and no doubt worrying for Malays and Klings, has put the fear of God into the Europeans. With the war in the Crimea in mind, people now clearly see that for their safety they cannot rely upon forces other than their own. And yet there are no British troops here other than a few Artillery, our military might consisting of Indian Artillery and Madras Sepoys. So last Saturday a public meeting was called, the Governor presiding, at which it was decided to form a permanent Volunteer Force amongst the European community, the 'Singapore Volunteer Rifle Corps'. Already about five dozen have signed up to serve, and the Governor has agreed to be its first Colonel. The way my uncle managed the violence has met with universal approval, and at the same meeting he was thanked profusely and presented with a sword of honour, a tribute he takes much to heart.

With this in mind it was with some misgivings that last Monday when out for my morning walk I was suddenly disturbed by the sound of gun-fire coming from the direction of the town. Hurrying home, I arrived at the same time as a message from Uncle Tom saying a man had run amok and was still on the prowl. Apparently a Bugis had rushed into town wielding a long dagger, a 'kris', in each hand and had seriously wounded a Chinaman. Luckily the Fort was nearby and soldiers were soon on the scene and fired at the man, but, although wounded, he escaped to the river where he threw one kris away and with the other gripped in his teeth plunged into the water. The soldiers followed by boat as best they could but it was an hour before they found him hiding below a bridge. At this, he rose with a roar and charged towards them but before they could fire, he dropped dead in the mud.

But I really must assure you that in general the Settlement seems most secure! Yes, we have had our riot and the occasional amok, but in fact the Europeans, whether men or women, feel quite at liberty to go where we will at any hour. Certainly, robberies do occur, but these are done stealthily and at night and never involve violence, and that is more than you can say for London Town. There are two prisons, but by far the larger, that below Government Hill, is filled with Indian and not home-grown convicts, whilst that for the latter, to the south of the town, is apparently far from crowded. The Malays seem a peaceable people and the Chinese generally well ordered, and I think for both that if crime occurs amongst them they usually find ways of dealing with it which do not involve our courts.

On a more cheerful note, I have been persuaded to join the cricket team. Do not assume, Harry, that this is an honour as it has to be said that *anyone* is welcomed, for to obtain 22 players of an evening is no easy matter. Nor should you think that I have suddenly become enamoured of the game but it is, at least in its pace, well suited to these tropic climes. But I admit to being mindful of the social potential, not that we have a fine club house but at least there is a tent for shelter and refreshment on the Plain where we play, and the players tend to be the more lively members of society.

There is no division between Gentlemen and Players – we are all both, from the redoubtable Mr

Read, always known as WH, who captains one side to myself, a far outfielder on the other. Our own captain is about my age but both of more exalted lineage and skill with bat and ball – Abu Bakar, the son of the Malay ruler. Abu, although a Mohammedan, has been to Mr Keasbury's school and is well versed in all things English, from tennis to Tennyson, and he is damned good at cricket. You will like him.

    Now I must leave you. This Sunday is a special Day of Prayer for the Russian War and I must assist my aunt whose turn it is to cheer our little chapel with flowers and greenery, a task not easily accomplished.

Your sporting friend in Singapore,

*Ben*

a game of cricket

Cemetery Gateway

*Sunday, 13 August 1854*

My dear Harry,

I am delighted to get your letter of the 22nd of June and pleased to know that you have received my account of the journey here. Just three months to receive an answer to my letters whereas in the early days, I am told, nine months would hardly have sufficed. Ah, the marvels of progress and the P & O!

And best of all is to know that your intention is still to come to Singapore. With this in mind we will now seek a suitable position for you, and when we find it I will ask Uncle to write to your father.

And so to my doings. As you well know, I am usually no church-goer, but from my last letter you will have learnt that I feel it necessary to attend on certain Sundays. Uncle is often, by good fortune, busy but my aunt wishes to go regularly and I feel it my duty to accompany her when he is unable. As my uncle admitted, with a twinkle in his eye and away from Mary's hearing: "You see, things here are ill-planned. The steamers from China and Calcutta seem frequently to arrive on a Sunday, which is in consequence a most busy day and thus I am, sadly, often prevented from attending church."

The walk to the chapel is merely a stone's throw, but entering it is pleasant, the interior cool and dim compared to the heat and glare outside. Now you will ask me, why 'chapel'. Surely a town with Singapore's pretensions should have a church, if not a cathedral? Well, it does have one, but they are knocking it down! I will tell you more of this later, so back to the chapel.

As it is small, two services are held each Sunday morning. Last Sunday I went to the second, and I suppose, as with meals, one should avoid the second sittings. The place was half empty, some already appearing asleep, the only animation being that of a couple of local boys who drew the long punkahs back and forth over the heads of the assembled worshippers. After a while there was a disturbance at the front, and a pale young lady entered with another local boy who immediately started pumping the organ enthusiastically. At this time the only ones who showed any enthusiasm for their lot were the three young pagans, but then the lady at the console started swaying animatedly and the organ pealed forth. This was the cue for the entry of the clergyman and his clerk. These two then presented us with Matins, the congregation remaining completely silent, our only animation being standing, sitting or kneeling as appropriate. The lessons were obscure and the sermon dull and full of the usual platitudes, but blessedly short. This over, the vicar gave a perfunctory blessing and he and his clerk scurried out, and none too soon we found ourselves hurrying home to lunch.

Now this is what I have learnt about our fine church and its destruction. St Andrew's was built less than 20 years ago, and by our finest architect (notice the 'our', Harry - you see, I belong already), a Mr Coleman who did many other notable buildings here in the '20s and '30s. I must say, it looks a rather dull structure to me, low and plain. Perhaps for that reason a tower and steeple were stuck on a few years later, and that was perhaps the place's undoing. Soon the tower was struck by lightening and nasty cracks appeared. And then it was struck again, and so a couple of years ago the whole place was boarded up and is now being demolished. So the English all have to go to worship at the Mission Chapel, the oldest Christian building in the town, though it is hoped that shortly a new church will be sanctioned.

I learned with some amusement from Lim that the boarding up distressed not only the English but many Chinese as well. This was not because of their Christian bent but rather because they thought that the place's abandonment was due to its haunting by evil spirits, that such spirits could only be appeased by the offering of human heads, and that these heads were being collected from the innocent at night by gangs of vicious convicts! Such is the origin of a 'head scare', a not uncommon myth when great buildings are built or boarded up. In this case a committee of the most venerable of the Chinese had to be set up to counteract the nonsense, but even the Great and the Good of the Celestials needed some weeks to work their magic.

Of the ways of the Chinese I have already told you a little, but should now tell you of their part of town, a place of such vibrancy and colour as will amaze you. The streets there, dense and narrow, are lined with terraces of what are best called shop-houses. These are two stories high, the entrance off the street being the shop and the remainder the house. The lower storey is cut away to give a covered path, the 'five-foot way' in front of the shop, the overhanging upper storey with its shuttered windows being support on stout pillars between which hang 'tatties', woven blinds, to shade the path. Built of brick plastered over and often painted pale blue or light yellow, the terraces are both practical and handsome.

The streets are further enhanced by wonderful sign-boards, each shop having jutting from its wall one or two large vertical boards of red or black on which are painted big Chinese characters in gold, and over the door a huge red lantern above a further colourful sign, and then red paper with inscriptions pasted to door-posts, lintels and window casings.

China Town

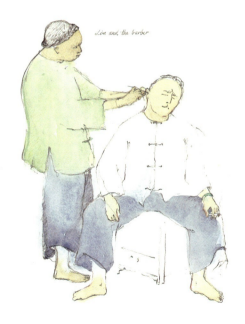

Lin and the barber

Water Carrier

Boy

Coolie

I have said that the Chinese speak a multitude of languages and this is true. But wonderfully, one written language can be read by all regardless of their province. This, blessedly, contains no alphabet or grammar, consisting solely of symbols each representing a single word. I suppose that this can be likened to Arabic numerals being spoken with such different sounds amongst the nations of Europe.

Now, add people to our scene, the coolie in his white and blue, the towkay in his silk, the Jew in rich dark robes, the Kling woman draped in scarlet. And overhead like the flags of all nations fly those same clothes, the family washing stretched on bamboo poles jutting from the upper windows. And everywhere the smell of incense, the noise of drums and bells, and the babbling, often shouting, of a dozen tongues!

Traders appear to group together, so blacksmiths are clustered on one street, carpenters on another, and elsewhere tin-workers, goldsmiths, butchers, bakers, crockery and opium sellers, coffin makers and money changers. Many ply their trade quite open to the streets, and you can watch cobblers and coopers, tailors and weavers hard at their work. Then there are the itinerant vendors, the Malays and Chinese with their goods on a shoulder stick and Klings with theirs on their heads, halting at their favourite pitch along the five-foot way to squat against a wall. Barbers and fortune-tellers, knife-sharpeners and locksmiths, and medicine-men to heal both physical and spiritual ailments. The best are the Chinese food-stalls, one end of the shoulder stick bearing a box containing a fire with a small copper cauldron for soup, and the other a basket with rice, noodles, cakes, and various vegetables and condiments. And, music to your ear Harry, Lim has instructed me how to get an excellent meal of three or four dishes for a mere three cents!

Lim himself will sometimes set up shop here of an evening writing letters for the illiterate, a task much in demand when a ship is to sail for China. I have once or twice joined him at his table to enjoy the busy scene. At a neighbouring pitch, an old Chinaman loudly berates any passers-by, inviting them, so I am told, to be relieved of any troublesome teeth. After a few minutes a Malay comes and takes the proffered seat, pointing to his mouth and talking animatedly. The dentist rummages in his bag for a while, withdraws a red plaster and claps it over the patient's cheek where the offending tooth is, while with the other hand he opens the man's mouth and inserts a small quantity of white paste. After a minute or two he withdraws his hands, picks up a formidable pair of pliers, sticks them in the open mouth and after a few deft movements whips out the tooth. But the most curious thing is no cry escapes the patient, nor can I detect on his face the slightest sign of pain. Yet the bleeding fang held up in triumph proves that the deed is done.

The shops along Boat Quay, where I work, are particularly exotic as they are chandlers and provide all the needs of the multitude of ships that visit Singapore. The largest of these is Whampoa's, about whose owner I should tell you more anon, where, behind all the hardware that any ship could want, lies a Noah's Ark of sheep, goats, pigs, poultry and pigeons in pens with various monkeys and parrots in cages, whilst below in pools swim ducks and geese. The noise occasioned by the crowing, bellowing, bleating and quacking is amazing, and the dirt produced, although reached by every tide, both plentiful and noxious.

And it is Whampoa who has brought us ice! It may not be obvious in London, particularly as winter approaches, what this substances means out here, but if I say that Mr Whampoa, as astute a business man as one could hope to find, has felt fit this year to start to import it from America, you will gain some idea. Ah, ice with our whiskys and our gins! But if it is thus welcomed by the gentry, it is the children who find it most exciting. Such amazing rock!

Once away from the main commercial streets, the terraces become solely of houses, the lower floor a series of halls. In front lies the reception hall with a central shrine to Kwan Yin, the Goddess of Mercy, and the household spirits, with tables and chairs against the walls, not used by the family except for worship but giving the visitor a good impression. Behind a screen lies the second hall to which friends can be admitted, and beyond that a third hall, the ancestral hall, only for the family and the closest of friends. Indeed, the women of the household seem to spend most of their time in the furthest hall for it is seldom that I see other than men and boys in the houses that I pass. In Lim's house I have so far penetrated as far as the second hall, the greatest pleasure there being the sight of his eldest sister who is quite lovely, neat and slim, her delicate face framed by the most wonderful hair, long, straight, black and shining. And such a smile, both shy and curious in equal proportions!

I suppose the most notable characteristic of the Chinese man, one that sets him apart from all others, is his tonsorial habit. The pigtail is universal amongst the men, rich and poor, young and old, nearly always most carefully tended, often decorated with intertwined coloured silks and usually hanging loose. At work, it may be wrapped around the head to keep it out of harm's way but it will always be released in the presence of a superior. And none will shave themselves but instead present themselves to a barber once a week. So barbers are plentiful, many carrying out their work on the sidewalks.

As I had previously expressed an interest in this work, Lim one morning asked me if I would like to accompany him on his regular visit. The barber he frequented, a young man but skilled at his profession, had his pitch along Tanjong Pagar road, a box for his instruments and a stool for his client being all his requirements. He kindly found another stool for me and I settled down to watch as Lim, removing his glasses, lit up a cigarette. First he took out a large razor, sharpened it quickly on a leather strop and proceeded to shave the top of Lim's head, using no soap or water. Then the razor was drawn down to where his whiskers would have been if Lim had not been Chinese, then across the throat, the cheeks, and even between eyebrow and eyelash. Laying down the razor he quickly undid the plait, combed the long hair which now fell almost to the pavement, rubbed some fluid into it with deft strokes of his hands, re-plaited it with new red silk thread, and finally coiling it neatly around Lim's head. Then, tilting back the head, he prised open my friend's mouth and went to work on his tongue with a rough wooden spatula and then on his teeth with a little sharpened stick, rinsing his instruments in a small cup of water. Then with a tiny pair of scissors he attacked some hairs bold enough to grow in the ears and nostrils, then, tilting Lim's head to either side, he gouged out his ears with little tweezers, rinsing these in the same bowl of water, and then attacked his finger nails, taking particular care over that on the little finger of the left hand which Lim allows to grow to a great length, an affectation universal amongst Chinese men, even labourers. When all was neat, the barber finally drew a bottle of scented water from a pocket and splashed it liberally about. Throughout, he had worked silently but, his task completed, he smiled broadly and broke into chatter. And little more than half an hour later and only a few cents poorer we were on our way again, at least one of us clean and smooth and fragrant.

You must forgive me if I seem to meander on but you must remember that the nights can sometimes be long, and anyway I enjoy the recording of pleasures, especially if they can help persuade you to join me. With that I must leave you, but not before wishing you much happiness on your birthday. Again we will be but a year apart. Remember, it is a Harry no older than 18 years of age that I wish to welcome to Singapore.

Your friend the Chinaman,

*Wednesday, 16 August 1854*

My dear friend,

Your letter of the fifth of July has come to hand with the terrible news about George. Oh Harry, I am indeed most sorry for you and your family. News of the Russian war filters through slowly, but we had been hearing good reports of our successes before your letter came. Now all is sorrow. I know how much you loved him, which I can fully understand from my own slight acquaintance. What can I say but that my thoughts are with you and your family.

I will write no more here, but may I say, with no reflection on your family's loss, that I hope that this will not affect your plans to join me here?

Your sorrowing friend,

*Ben*

Ang Kim Cheok

*Tuesday, 26 September 1854*

My dear Harry,

Firstly I must tell you the good news – that my uncle has promise of a position for you here similar to mine, working as a clerk for Boustead & Company! This will, I know, suit you admirably, and we then can together explore the possibilities of combining our talents and our energies in some new enterprise. Uncle is to write to your father and will I am sure persuade him of the opportunities here for his youngest offspring.

The mail from London dispatched on the 8th of August reached us on the 11th of this month, four days before it was due, and at 34 days a record. Everyone here is most pleased and the usual complaints about the P & O have somewhat abated. It seems that in the far flung outposts of empire mail has an importance which it can never carry in a metropolis. We all await its arrival with almost unseemly enthusiasm, and all our writings, and much else besides, are timed by the mail flags, red for departure to Europe, Calcutta blue, China yellow and Australia white.

And this time my unseemly enthusiasm was amply rewarded – a fine letter from you, as well as one from my father. It is good to hear that you are all coming to terms with your great loss, and indeed seeing the nobility of George's death. He clearly approached the dangers of war as he did all things, with energy and humour. You and your family have great cause to be proud.

How kind to say that you are sure that Mr de Sousa will have met his match in Mr Cook. And that my letters generally amuse you for, as they are written in snatches as time allows, I had feared that this might not be so. Yet you say that, riots and all, they are indeed persuading you to come to Singapore. At this I am delighted! And to turn the screw: as winter approaches, remember the bitter one we huddled through last year? As the fogs roll in, ponder my predicament under the tropic sun, and resolve to make this the last you will suffer for some years.

And talking of the mail, I must digress to tell you how Benjamin took a swim in our river, saved the mail and lived to tell the tale. One of the minor peculiarities of the place, but one which exercises our merchants greatly, is that Commercial Square and the Post Office are on opposite banks of the river. Of course, the original planners, seeing the huge importance attached to the mail by the women here, many of whom appear to organize their lives around mail days, may have considered having the Post Office on the European bank sensible. But then the greatest volume of mail is generated by commerce. A footbridge near the mouth of the river has long been mooted but nothing yet decided so a frequent sampan service still ferries mail bags and passengers across. This I have often taken, always without mishap until last week when, for no reason I could discern, I and my fellow passengers and mail suddenly found ourselves immersed in the fetid waters, the boat bottom up beside us. As we were more than half way across the shore was close and for this I struck out on my back, mouth firmly shut and dragging with one hand a mail bag and with the other a young girl who seemed to be struggling somewhat. No damage was sustained by any of the passengers which could not be righted by lengthy ablutions. And one of my fellow clerks, Wan Eng Kiat, has kindly taken my watch to dry it out as he is apparently a wizard with these things.

You say that I seldom mention the ladies in my narrative, and that may be true. The fact is that few are to be seen. The European mems and girls seem seldom to leave their homes, and when they do are conveyed hither and yon in carriages. Likewise the natives keep their women folk largely secluded behind doors, so that the streets, shops, markets and wharves are largely peopled by men, the gentler sex being only in abundance at parties or the most public of gatherings such as the Esplanade of which I have spoken. But then I must admit to you, when there on Friday last, what caught my eye was no fair lady but a Chinaman in the smartest of phaetons pulled by a spirited pair, the young fellow most beautifully dressed in a suit of light tweed, with buckskin gloves and fashionable soft grey hat, with his long pigtail hanging down behind. On closer examination I saw that it was Ang Kim Cheak, who has recently inherited his father's business in Philip Street and is now one of our Chinese notables. I have on occasion had lunch with him, unremarkable in his working clothes, but arrayed thus, as dashing and handsome as he is rich.

Here I must add that my aunt is again with child, swelling nicely and apparently enjoying her predicament. But I fear, Harry, that it is not necessarily such respectable ladies that you wish to hear about. And Singapore, being the great port that it is, does of course provide the sailor with all his needs. Thus there are streets which at night teem with more feminine talent than can be seen in the whole town during daylight hours, and I will admit to you that I have repaired there once or twice in the company of friends. If you are satisfied with black hair and brown eyes, everything is available that a man can desire. Certainly it is my good fortune that blond hair and blue eyes are the greatest rarity here and thus a great attraction. For myself, I favour the Chinese girls, their slight forms and round

Miss Oxley

faces, their enthusiasm; and they are – how can I put it to spare your blushes – delightfully active! But you may prefer the dusky Klings, tall and graceful, who can more fiercely teach you eastern ways. However it is, my friend, please be assured that this place can meet even your insatiable desires.

And now to a different talent. You will of course have heard of Sir James Brooke, Rajah of Sarawak. Well, I have met him! He is in Singapore for an enquiry, but I am finding it difficult to find out what the enquiry is really about as all I speak to call it a nonsense and tell me it is about nothing! Anyway, I met him at Mr Read's house where he is staying. This is the WH of our cricket team, one of our many Scotch worthies and a firm friend of the Rajah, and to his house we repaired on Sunday the 10th for a gathering he had arranged for Sir James on the eve of the enquiry's opening.

The Rajah is not tall and looks older and more worn than I had expected, but he has a charm and sparkle about him which all can see. It is remarkable to think, looking at him, that this man has gone to a distant land such as Borneo and has there, single-handed, carved for himself a kingdom. And by all accounts this kingdom is now both peaceful and prosperous, and its ruler loved by his people. That is a tale of Empire for you! But even on the briefest acquaintance you can sense the power and purpose of the man. And, further to charm me, although well known and at the gathering surrounded by many of the gentry of the place, he found time to talk to me with sincerity and grace. Yet he is clearly worried about the proceedings, not that the case will go against him as he is convinced of the rightness of his actions, but rather that it will harm his standing and thus his government. Furthermore, as he had left many of his staff ill in Sarawak he was thus even more loathe to spend time in this place.

Let me try to piece together what I have learnt about this enquiry. It is all to do either with pirates or with politics depending on the point of view. Apparently, some five years ago off Sarawak a native fleet was destroyed by a force, arranged by Sir James, of Naval and Company vessels. All here know that pirates of various descriptions abound in these seas, and this is not just from the Europeans for the local people speak of it too. And in Sarawak, it is not solely his charm that makes the Rajah loved but the fact that he has stamped on piratical attacks, giving the people the security in which they can prosper. Hence the fight against the native fleet which was a marauding one, and hence the death of some 500 people. I am told that accusations against the Rajah and the Navy began at home soon after the battle though I never heard of them. But Hume and Cobden and their ilk made out in Parliament that Sir James was some sort of tyrant who enjoyed killing peaceful peasants, and this was spurred on by papers both in London and in Singapore. Here, the *Straits Times* took the accusers' side and the *Free Press* Sir James', and a fine time was had by all.

But why, years later, is there a Commission? Well, according to Mr Read, it is all politics – and he and many others here are angry about it. Apparently, when last year Lord Aberdeen became PM he proposed a Commission simply to secure the votes of Hume and his friends. This will certainly not surprise you, with your gloomy view of politics and politicians. Anyway, we will have to wait to see how it all pans out.

Having mentioned our press, I should here say a little more about it. The *Straits Times* is the newest and published each fortnight, but due to the antics of its editor, Mr Woods, at the Commission, I now rather favour its rival, the *Free Press*, which has been going twice as long and comes out twice as often. This was founded twenty years ago by Mr Napier, another Scot and another worthy, the first of the lawyers of Singapore and, with certain airs and graces, known beyond his hearing as 'Royal Billy', but he is a friend of many, and certainly of the Rajah of Sarawak.

As to piracy, it surely occurs and remains the curse of these waters, although less frequent now than a few years ago. The coming of steamers has helped for these are not beholden to the winds and are as fast as the fastest rowing boat. Remember that we may expect this year over a thousand square-rigged boats and well over twice that number of native boats to visit Singapore, so the pickings in neighbouring seas are rich. The Malays seem to indulge in piracy as a simple way of making a living, and it has taken much persuasion, not all of it merely verbal, to teach them otherwise. And many in the Dutch Indies remain unpersuaded. A favourite prize is the Chinese junk coming down on the monsoon, rich with goods for trade and men for slaves. But the Chinese themselves have their own pirates, who the English view less sympathetically as merely thieves. I have sometimes seen their so-called 'fast boats' in the harbour, these over a hundred feet long and pulled by at least sixty oars in two tiers, scampering over the waves like some giant centipede. But it is rumoured when away from the town these strange boats, which can sail and pull with equal facility, do not always obtain their merchandise by legal means.

The beach in front of the Chinese town is a hive of activity to rival the river basin, boats landing and setting forth, others being repaired, goods bought and sold, Malays plaiting ropes, Bugis making their great mat sails, and amongst it all children playing and swimming. Here at Telok Ayer many a

*Fast Boat*

grateful voyager has first set foot on Singapore and so the street above has many shrines where thanks can duly be offered. At either end are two for the Mohammedans from the south of India, the Chulias, one a rather plain mosque, the other a strange structure rather like an upturned table, and an elaborate one at that, a shrine to some god, Nagore Durgha. But it is in the centre that the most marvellous place is seen, a Chinese temple of curved roofs and quiet courtyards, of candles wreathed in incense smoke, of bells and drums, of fierce stone gods and smiling golden Buddhas. This is the Temple of Heavenly Bliss, Thian Hock Keng, as colourful and lively a place of worship, and as aptly named, as you could hope to find in a month of Sundays.

Today the temple is crowded with people, all going about their business independent of each other, arriving and departing when they will, talking animatedly or prostrating themselves in silence, lighting incense sticks or burning golden papers, all as different as can be from a well ordered English church. We enter through a fine doorway guarded by a herd of fierce beasts, tigers and lions and nasty looking warriors. The place is not a single building but rather a walled compound with splendid halls set amongst spacious courtyards. The central temple, flanked by two lesser buildings, is a shrine to the Goddess of the Sea, Ma Cho Po. Her statue, which came here from China itself, is flanked on either side by large images of jolly looking old men, sages I am told, and in front to left and right are two more figures but this time of horrible aspect, to frighten off evil. Over all stand two enormous red silk umbrellas beautifully embroidered in gold. On a central table are huge brass urns to hold incense sticks, candles, and flowers in vases, these all replenished by the worshippers. Here Lim and his sister light some sticks and prostrate themselves, she as lovely as ever bent thus, her hair spread around her on the tiles.

Sights of an altogether less elevated nature can also surprise in this surprising place. Two weeks ago I went shooting with a cousin of WH, Bob Read, and his Malay servant Kasim off the Serangoon Road. Beyond Bukit Selegie, commonly known as the Rockies and a fine place for a picnic, the land becomes quite swampy. Here snipe abound and the sport is usually good. We left our ponies by the racecourse and struck out past the Hindu burial grounds to the woodland, a less than pleasant place to walk for, in contrast to the high forest, the vegetation is low and remarkable thorny, and the ground muddy. We had not gone far, keeping to the slight ridges which are drier, when we came upon a clearing in which three bodies lay, partly cremated. Two were charred to cinders, but on the other the fire had evidently gone out and he was only slightly grilled and smelling horribly. Clearly animals had attempted to consume what the flames had not, for one of his legs and part of his right arm lay some distance away, partly devoured. On seeing this, Kasim retired precipitately by the path on which we had come, saying later that it was their ghosts and not their corpses that had concerned him. Bob and I pretended curiosity to each other, but in fact the sight and the smell quite put us off our stride, and soon we persuaded ourselves that the day was too hot and the game too sparse to continue.

Thian Hock Keng Temple

Nagore Durgha Shrine

Banana Tree

Malay tops

And then on my return and not far from home I had a tremendous spill in the street. A wretched pariah dog started chasing the pony and somehow got under his feet and threw him down. I was hurled off and hit the ground with a tremendous thump, and was dreadfully shaken. Some kind passers-by came to my rescue and then caught dobbin, and after a rest we continued on our way. Those wretched dogs remain much too numerous – and this despite the fact that every week convicts are sent out to kill as many as they can.

On a more cheerful note, I have since I last wrote attended with considerable pleasure as fine a society wedding as we can hope for here. I know that you enjoy Captain Marryat's novels and it was his daughter, Florence, apparently also a novelist, who was wedded to the son of Mr Church, the Resident Councilor or judge. The Church's house is next to St Andrews on the Esplanade, a perfect location for such an event you may think, but then of course the church is boarded up so the service was in the Mission Chapel and the celebrations later at their house. I must say that the English here know how to celebrate in style, helped perhaps by the lack of onerous work and the abundance of servants. Certainly that evening a vast feast was consumed, washed down by barrels of wine, all accompanied by music and dancing far into the night. Stimulated by all this a group of us, all unmarried, then repaired to the town to sample the delights that eventual marriage will bring.

For exercise of an entirely respectable nature I have started playing fives, introduced to it by my rich friend Kim Cheak. This is a strange game, very English I am told but new to me and, I expect, to you. My quarrel with it is that it is played indoors and is most energetic, so that it is hardly suitable for this climate. By the river we have some courts, each small and walled all around. Within this two of us stand, or rather leap in all directions, belting a small ball from wall to wall and floor with gloved hands. My pleasure from it, apart from the healthy sweat, is that only the nicest people play it. Yes, I will teach you when you come. Kim Cheak is both fit and tall and a devil at it but his eyesight restrains him, and I am confident that with a little more practice he will have met his match in Benjamin Cook.

And with that, your well exercised friend must end, wishing you and your family every good wish.

Red Dutch Building in Malacca

*Friday, 27 October 1854*

My dear Harry,

For the first time since I arrived I have left the Settlement! Some weeks ago Mr Carnie for whom I work informed me that he would have to visit Penang and wished me to accompany him which I readily accepted. The company has an office and go-down there and as accounts will soon be due he wished to visit to check books and inventory. I had of course seen the island on my way to Singapore but then we had hardly gone ashore, so I looked forward to linger there, and indeed to the journey as well. The little steamer *Hooghly*, which does this journey each week, was to convey us, and we were to sail on Sunday the 15th of last month and be gone 12 days. By mid morning the passengers and baggage were all on board, ready for departure at noon, and soon we were steaming westwards through the islands that I had last seen upon my arrival seven months ago. About 2 o'clock in the afternoon the captain had gone below to take his siesta, and many of the ship's crew and passengers had done the same. I myself had just settled down on the deck when we were suddenly disturbed by a violent shock on the starboard side. After a short grinding passage the ship stopped and then toppled heavily to port, and there she lay with her starboard paddle box clean out of the water, fixed on what we soon discovered to be a coral reef. For several minutes the place was complete pandemonium, every hatch disgorging bewildered passengers and crew who all milled around aimlessly, the Captain running backwards and forwards amongst them muttering "Jesus Christ!", and apparently quite unable to credit the fact that we were upon a rock. After a little time some order was restored, and we had noticed that fortunately we were on a rising tide. So slowly the poor *Hooghly* came upright again, and when both paddles were safely in the water the engines were started and, with some further grinding, we were backed off the rock and were on our way again.

The passage to Malacca took about a day, somewhat longer than planned due to our mishap.

Penang Hill

There we stopped briefly to unload some goods and exchange some passengers. The oldest of the three Settlements, but now the least, it looks a pretty place, a quiet harbour backed by a hill with fort and church, a relic of the days of the Portuguese. Behind lies the ever present forest and in the distance Mount Ophir, a mountain of some size. A place for a quiet convalescence perhaps, but not to live. I wonder how long it will be until we have a steam train available to take us up to Malacca, to Penang and beyond to Siam?

Penang itself is a further day's steaming, and it was not until Tuesday evening that we were safely anchored in the roads and ready to go ashore. The harbour is a fine one, the town lying on a point and colourful from the sea, with large hills ranged behind. This was the first of our settlements in the Straits, a Captain Light nobly playing the role that Raffles was later to play with greater effect in Singapore. The town's comparative eclipse seems nothing to do with the founder nor with the place as such, this island being certainly as attractive as the one to the south, but solely to location.

We were entertained that night by Mr Vaughan and his young wife with whom we were to stay. Mr Vaughan has the same job in Penang as my uncle enjoys in Singapore, superintending the police, and he is a great friend of Uncle Tom's and thinks the world of him. Like many others who have settled here he spent his early life at sea, part of it on the good ship *Hooghly*! Well, the next days were spent on inventory work of whose dullness you will be well aware, but relief was at hand. Mr Vaughan has a bungalow on the hill and it had been arranged that we were to spend the weekend there. Mr Carnie was as eager as I for this treat and he arranged for us to finish our work early on the Friday. Mr and Mrs Vaughan were to accompany us and in the late afternoon we took a gharry for the four or so miles to the foot of the hill. There we exchanged the carriage for chairs and were carried aloft at a great pace. The distance from the foot of the hill to the flag-staff is about 3 miles and the ascent 2,400 feet, and we made this within the hour!

Dusk was falling as we reached the bungalow which was finely placed on a ridge. To the east there was a magnificent view of the town and the mainland of Province Wellesley whose rich plains stretch many miles until they are lost in mountainous ranges. To the west the sky was changing rapidly from orange to red as the sun sank beneath the horizon, and soon it was dark and we went in to dress for dinner. The town, like Singapore, is always hot but the hill enjoys temperatures at least 10 degrees cooler. So as night fell a fire was lit in the hearth, and later in bed I pulled a blanket over me, the first fire and blanket for many a month.

The next morning I awoke to find the hill enveloped in mist. Through the mist the nearer trees could be glimpsed, feathery tree-ferns and shrubs gnarled by the wind, and from beyond came the hootings of monkeys and the cries of birds. It was very lovely, cool and quiet and unlike anything I had seen so far in the East.

*Penang Hill Flora*

The cook provided me with some sustenance before the others were astir, and I set off to enjoy this strange new world. But as the sun rose so the mists dispersed and soon I was back in the Penang of yesterday, the world laid at my feet.

By Sunday, thoroughly refreshed, Mr Carnie, Mr Vaughan and I resolved to walk back to the town, and thus we set off after lunch, dropping down through ever taller forest to ever greater heat. On the way, perhaps to emphasise the delights of our walk, they regaled each other and myself with tales of the horrors of Batavia which they both had apparently visited much too often, warning me most strongly against ever being tempted to venture thither. The place itself is apparently completely cheerless, situated in a swamp and a veritable hotbed of malaria and other plagues, so Europeans have chosen to reside entirely in the country, about 3 or 4 miles further on. Worse still, the office hours are strange so an Englishman exiled to Batavia must learn to live like a Dutchman, with breakfast at 6 am, a five hour working day, and dinner soon after noon. And to compound these horrors is the food, and my companions' indignation grew as they described the Dutch dinner, the infamous "rijstafel" or rice-table, which they considered was a textbook of excess although I thought it sounded rather delicious. Apparently it is a plate of rice upon which you pour vegetable curry and then various meats and fishes, and all sorts of pickles and things from little dishes, and then, staggering to your place with this immense heap, you mix the whole lot together with fork and spoon and consume the resulting mud-coloured mound. After this comes more meat, then dessert, coffee and fruit, whereupon it is necessary to retire to bed for an hour or two. Perhaps you and I should, after all, contrive a visit to Batavia?

And so we reached the town and a well earned bath and dinner with, to my regret, no rijstafel. Then a couple of days to complete our work, and on Wednesday to the *Hooghly* again to carry us, this time uneventfully, once more to Singapore. We had been gone 12 days.

There has been much to do at the office since our return and my writing to you has been somewhat delayed. But I hope that this tale of my little adventure will further strengthen your resolve to travel hither.

Let me end here with another of the sights of Singapore which so amuse me, this concerning the many uses of the Chinaman's tail. One morning in a street I saw two men arguing loudly when one grabbed his own tail and started to whip the other with it, whereupon his opponent commenced a similar assault, the two now leaping around most athletically with fearsome shouts as they struck at each other, much to the delight of the crowd that had quickly gathered. And on another morning I saw a policeman leading two men towards the station, the pigtail of one knotted firmly to that of the other so that they walked side by side like lovers.

And what of displays of true affection here? They are certainly more readily seen than at home, at least for and amongst the young. Babies are held and cosseted by both mother and father alike. If a child cries it will be picked up and hugged, and even if it willfully misbehaves it will seldom be scolded. Does this spoil the child as our parents would have us believe? All I can say is that to all appearances the children here are both well behaved and contented, and that in later life the people are hard working and certainly as cheerful as at home. Even the English children seem content for, although their parents may behave as at home, here the amah will pick them up if they cry and indulge them if they are unhappy.

On the street boys and young men can be seen walking hand in hand. Of course girls, and all women, are scarce in public, but this is not the reason; rather it is that if friends, they are happy to show it. But amongst adults, even husband and wife, an open display of affection seems as rare here as in England, more's the pity.

In closing, let me wish you and your family the very merriest of Christmases and a most happy and prosperous new year, a year in which we will meet again in tropical lands.

From your most affectionate friend,

*Sunday, 12 November 1854*

Dear Harry,

In your last letter you asked after my health, perhaps thinking that I am keeping the dreadful illnesses of the place, fevers and poxes, from you for fear of dissuading you of the joys of joining me. But the reason I have remained silent is that my health has remained rude. Until, that is, a few days ago when I came down with some fever. Mary, fearing malaria, called the doctor, but as the fever was not of a cyclical nature he thought it from another cause but dosed me thoroughly with quinine none the less. Thereafter it abated and now I am feeling much better though somewhat weakened, but, with time on my hands, certainly strong enough to write to you.

To comfort you if you fear for your health in these tropical parts, I should say that we are well provided with doctors. The Dunmans call upon Dr Little, the best known of our practitioners and of course Scotch. He is one of three brothers in the Settlement, all pillars of the community, respectable and hard working, as befits those whose grandfather was a Highland minister and father an Edinburgh lawyer. Robert is the eldest and practices with Dr Allen in the Square, where he lives. He is the backbone of the Library, the Presbyterian congregation, the St Andrews Day committee, and is the Coroner! His forebears would be proud of him, and justly. Whereas Robert opened a private hospital for seamen a few years ago, his brothers, John and Matthew, have last year opened our finest emporium, John Little & Company, sensibly leaving the doing of good to the eldest and instead concentrating upon the making of money.

As you surmise, the climate here is always hot and wet for we lie only 90 miles from the Equator, but you must not think this very oppressive. Certainly at night, enveloped in a net to keep off the mosquitoes, and particularly if with a fever, it is hardly fresh, but the early mornings are often pleasantly cool as it also is after a rain storm. The rains come usually in the afternoon, all too often when I am

Dugis trader

fish

shells

Tembusu

Spathoglottis Plicata

out and about my business. And what storms they can be, the clouds towering overhead in billow upon billow grey and white, and lit from within by great flashes of yellow and sometimes orange lightening, the thunder crashing all around and the rain coming down in torrents. From a sheltering doorway I view the deserted street, the washing hanging sodden from its poles, the shop signs now empty of colour swinging in the wind. And then the rain eases and as the sky lightens colour returns to the street, and I scurry on my way.

I have said that we do not have seasons here, that it is always hot and damp, but now I learn that I am mistaken. Not about the heat and dampness but about the winds. Last month, as you were enjoying autumn, the winds here changed. Before, indeed, I had hardly noticed them but am told that they were from the south-west and these allowed trade from the east, from Borneo, Manila and the Celebes. Now they have turned north-east and are stronger, and this monsoon brings heavier rain and also the ships from the north, from China, Siam and Cochin-China.

The Bugis traders from the Celebes are perhaps the most colourful that are welcomed here, their boats most picturesque, two-masted and striped black and white along their sides. The men are muscular fellows, wild looking, dressed in short drawers with a cloth thrown over a shoulder like a plaid. These are the great traders of the archipelago, and now as the winds turn many visit us both to seek shelter and to do business, their coming causing a considerable stir. Each boat soon sets up shop on Telok Ayer beach, and many people repair there to see parrots and parakeets, spices and sandalwood, coffee and camphor, shells and sarongs, gold dust and pearls, birds' nests and turtles' eggs, and hard is the bargaining and bartering. Imagine if you can, as you gaze upon the fading trees by Father Thames, the beach scene, the little shelters made of palm leaves, the Bugis brown and wild with their exotic wares, the throng of local people, a Chinese woman dressed in black, her children plump and succulent, a Kling wife a riot of colour, a stately Arab in flowing robes calmly bargaining, Malay boys chasing amongst the stalls with round laughing faces. Then you might get a taste of life by the water here.

As dusk falls, people start to wend their way home and lamps come on in house and street. From the shore the houses along Beach Road look very fine, light flooding the tall white pillars of the upper storeys which jut above the garden shrubberies. Doors and windows are thrown open to admit the evening breeze and within can be seen the residents gathered at table or relaxing with a drink. And in the dense town, for most the day's work is also done though for others it is just beginning. As shutters are pulled across shop fronts, so other smaller doors open. Inside one you may glimpse men reclining with long stemmed pipes, in another a group bent low beneath a lamp, the rapid click-clack-click telling a game of Chinese checkers is in progress. And at a third, a young lady hovers by the opening, beckoning with her eyes.

The Chinese appear to spend most of their waking hours working or eating,

pipe

basket

China Town

bowl of noodles

but there are two vices which they are happy to indulge in publicly, gambling and the smoking of opium. Gaming can be seen everywhere; in shops, under the colonnades, in markets, at the corner of almost any street, crowds gather around the gaming tables. And at festivals gambling replaces working so that it is then gaming and eating that seem solely to occupy them.

The smoking of tobacco is a popular past-time amongst both men and women, but only the men indulging in opium. I have sought Lim's advice as to the joys of the drug, but although he admits to gaming he claims never to have smoked, fearing that it would harm his brain, by which he sets much store, and rightly. But I have persuaded him to take me to a shop and there explain the goings-on. The drug is sold in pieces about the size of a small pea, and with it are provided a pipe, a lamp, and a couch to lie on. The pipe is fitted with a metal lid with a central hole, and on this hole the opium ball is placed. The couches, raised benches about four feet wide, are in pairs with a passage between. The smokers lie facing the passage, their heads on pillows, and light the ball from a lamp placed between them. A ball lasts only a few seconds and perhaps eight are smoked before the fellow lays down the pipe and drifts away to some Chinese paradise.

Earlier, I told you about the Commission here that has been examining the conduct of Sir James Brooke in Sarawak. So one day about a month ago I asked leave to attend as its progress is much in the news, and this I did with Charlie Allan. He is again in Singapore, between visits to Malacca and to Borneo. The proceedings are in the Court House, a barn-like building lying between the river and the High Street, hemmed in by other buildings and a ship-yard so both airless and noisy. I wonder why the public buildings here are so poor – the Governor in a thatched roof bungalow, the Law in a barn of a Court House, the English Church a crumbling ruin, and the only public hall dilapidated. Perhaps it is that all is dedicated to Commerce, the merchants loathe to relinquish any of their profits in taxes, and the Government in distant India uncaring.

The Commission is conducted by two commissioners, assist by our Registrar, Mr Kerr. The commissioners are a strange pair, sitting solemnly behind their large desk. Both are from India, Mr Prinsep a lawyer and Mr Devereux a civil servant. The former is ancient, sometimes seems asleep, and when fully awake usually rambles away quite unnecessarily. The other is much sharper, with a fine sarcastic turn of phrase which generally fails to hide his obvious belief in the absurdity of the proceedings. During the day in question, Mr Woods who has led the opposition to Sir James as editor of the *Straits Times* was not even in court, this generally considered rather poor conduct. But the most surprising feature was the number of worthy citizens who said they had put their name to a memorial which condemned Sir James' actions believing that in fact it was in his favour! Keep this in mind when you are rich and famous and your signature is sought to some memorial – read it first! But I did feel sorry for some of them – poor Captain Wright of the *Hooghly* was much embarrassed to admit his signature as he well knows the reality of pirates and is a great admirer of Sir James. Anyway, there is general agreement that the case against the Rajah has broken down and that his actions will be fully exculpated.

Now from my bed of woe I must end this missive to my friend in darkest England. Please be assured that long before you read this your friend will be his usual boisterous self.

Trusting your health is good, I remain, my dear Harry, the soon to be boisterous

*Singapore Rhododendron*

To Harry, my dear friend,
with every good wishes
Don

*Sunday, 24 December 1854*

Dear Harry,

My first Christmas far from home, and I am thinking of my family and friends there and wishing all much happiness in the year to come. And for you yourself a long, exciting voyage – to Singapore! I wonder how it is in England; fierce weather, snow? Here it is hot as always but as the rains are now more frequent not as hot as before. Indeed today it has rained almost without ceasing which, with no work to attend, provides a fine excuse for putting pen to paper.

Your letter of the 20th of October is to hand, and it is fine to hear that your family has recovered somewhat from your terrible loss, and particularly that Helen is to become engaged. That must be a comfort to your parents with George no longer with you. And you have been to the Crystal Palace at its new home. How fortunate – I had so wished to do that before I left England but, alas, had no time for it.

And no, Lim does not write my letters for me. And no, a pigtail will not suit you – you will just have to be content with that scruffy brown mop. By the way, I will enclose with this a sketch I have done of my good self specially for you and your family so that at the year's end you are properly reminded of your handsome friend!

Be assured that I am again as fit as the proverbial fiddle and eager to tell you of my further adventures here in Singapore, starting with a rather special excursion. Some weeks ago Sir James Brooke sent me a note to ask if I would join him for a picnic. An honour I believe and a pleasure for, as I am sure you can sense, our Rajah has rather won my heart. So I accepted with alacrity. Picnicking is a great hobby of the place, and a proper one is no mere snack but a repast to rival those we indulge in indoors. I suppose that the warmth and humidity of the climate have much to do with it as outdoor pursuits are all the more attractive if leisurely, and then they indulge our love of a decent feast.

We met after lunch at 1 o'clock along the quay, Sir James and one of his staff from Sarawak called Charles Grant, Bob Read whom I have mentioned before, the son of our sort of Sultan, the cricketer Abu Bakar, and then two Chinamen, fives-player Kim Cheak whose late father was a friend of the Rajah and one unknown to me, Tan Beng Swee. These with myself and two boatmen made nine, all well laden with provision baskets and fishing gear. You would have enjoyed the company, none much older than us save the Rajah who proved, as the day wore on, to be as young in heart. Charles Grant I had not met before, a most lively and amusing fellow, a Scot but far from dour, and clearly no mere assistant but a dear friend of the Rajah. The passage to our chosen destination, a small island off the southern shore, was a short one and within the hour we had landed on what proved to be little more than a large sand-bar with shrubs and trees crowded along its crest, the tallest like thin fir trees, but many having splendidly large leaves and thus providing plentiful shade. There we set down our supplies and went off to swim and fish while the boatmen gathered firewood.

The sea here is of course most perfect for swimming. By any shore where there is a beach and not mangroves the water is calm, without currents and beautifully clear. There are certainly some nasty things to avoid, the most prevalent being a very unpleasant stinging jelly-fish, but sharks, which I had expected, are rare though sometimes their fins can be seen amongst the vessels in the harbour, perhaps attracted there by all the garbage thrown overboard. Here we splashed happily about, Sir James as full of mischief as the youngest of us, clearly delighted to be far from the cares of office and society. Then off to try our hand at fishing which did not prove easy, at least for me. But we all obtained something, Kim Cheak and the Rajah proving the most adept. The Rajah was delighted to find a Cook amongst the party but, with much laughter, he soon was persuaded of my culinary ignorance. Luckily others were adept with pan and fire so that when darkness fell, and fall it does at this latitude with remarkable swiftness, we had a catch of reasonable size and remarkable variety sizzling away. These, fish, crabs and shellfish, together with fresh vegetables, Chinese buns, chicken cutlets, sausages, cabinet pudding, preserved ginger and fruit *ad libitum*, all washed down with beer, made a fine repast. Then cigarettes were passed around and we had some songs, I regaling the company with *The Vicar of Bray* and our school song which, as you will no doubt be thinking, probably proved more stimulating to me than to my listeners. Soon the active day, the food and the drink took their toll and we embarked for home, the boatmen rowing us through calm waters, a quieter crew than that which had set out 12 hours before. I was not in my bed until 3 in the morning after an excursion I will long remember with the greatest pleasure.

The Commission being concluded, Sir James departed earlier this month for his beloved Sarawak, a good crowd of supporters being at Johnstone's pier to wish him farewell. The last I saw of him was at the St Andrew's Day dinner. As there are so many Scotch here, it is of no surprise that that day is celebrated in some style. For many years there was a ball, and it was generally thought of as one of the

Sand Dollar

crab

Picnic Island

Keling

Starfish

finest of the year. But recently, since the Assembly Rooms have become so dilapidated, it is merely a dinner held in the house of one of the Scotch worthies. Last year it was Dr Little's turn and next year it will be Captain Scott's, but this year it was the turn of Mr Carnie for whom I work which was nice as he has a fine place at Cairnhill to the west of the town, most suitable for a celebration. Being held on the 2nd, a Saturday, it was well attended and continued into the 'wee hours' as the Scotch would say. Of course the drink flowed well and I had, as they say, a most merry time, particularly as my friends suggest that our way home should be by the Chinese town where we found our favourites still awake and eager to please. A most satisfactory conclusion.

But being Christmas I should raise our sights to things higher than these gross pleasures. Certainly it has given me cause for thought to celebrate this great Christian feast in a place where the English church plays such a minor part in the religion of the people. Here, a plethora of gods are worshipped in a plethora of places, Christian, Jewish, Mohammedan, Hindu and Chinese. As I pass St Andrew's falling into ruins I am mindful of other places of worship now rising from the ground: a new temple for the Klings off the Serangoon Road, and the wooden mosque in Kampong Malacca rebuilt in brick.

Apart from our little chapel, Protestants can repair to Mr Keasbury's church on Prinsep Street, commonly called the Malay Chapel, and just this year a committee of the Scotch has agreed to raise the necessary funds to secure a minister from Scotland. Yet in this British possession it is the Roman Catholics who are more active in their belief. Their fine Church of the Good Shepherd was completed some years ago and is standing unstruck by lightening and busy with people, mainly Chinese, and they have turned their old church into an active school. Then there is the Portuguese church built only last year with Father Vicente de Santa Catharina in charge, who is as fine in figure as in name, a new Convent run by four nuns newly arrived from Penang, very black and very French, and of course the Chinese parish at Bukit Timah in the centre of the island where earlier I stayed.

But best of all for Christians is the Armenian Church, a delightful building which would indeed grace any London street, the delight deriving from its architecture rather than its function. Mr Coleman has designed many of the finest buildings in the settlement for the Rich and the Good, and in the Armenian Church he has surpassed himself. Outside it appears as a rectangular and classical building, heavily porticoed on three sides, to which only last year a fine tower and spire have been added. But it is upon entering it that one is particularly surprised and delighted for one finds that the main space, the nave, is in fact completely circular with a semi-circular chancel to the east. When you are here, although I know nothing of their religion, we will attend and test the acoustics of the place.

And, being Christmas, let us not forget the Jews. We have a small number here as I suppose in all parts of the world where business is to be conducted. They have a little synagogue in the Chinese town, just a shop-house that they use, and it is here that you may see their patriarch Abraham Solomon

Armenian Church

who not only leads their community in this promised land but indeed looks exactly as I am sure Moses looked – tall with long flowing robes, a turban and a great white beard. He apparently much likes to entertain but since he cannot eat with Christians and speaks no English the evenings at his house on Boat Quay, which I have not yet enjoyed, are somewhat unusual. Luckily his children have no such inhibitions and so it falls to them to entertain the guests.

You will have heard the name 'Coleman' now a number of times, so I should tell you a little more about him. Of course the town is indelibly stamped with the mark of Stamford Raffles who not only decreed its Free Trade nature but also outlined its physical form. But Raffles' outline of communities and streets was made material by an architect, one George Coleman, and he you also see everywhere. There he is on Government Hill, in many of the elegant mansions lining the streets below, in the handsome go-downs along the river, in the round market, in the delightful Armenian church, and, less admirably, in the dilapidated St Andrew's, a failure not only structurally but, to my mind, aesthetically. Sadly, he died here some ten years ago, quite young and with a new wife and son.

For structural failures, people here delight to talk of Major Faber who has now left the Settlement. The Major arrived from India in the early Forties as Superintending Engineer for the Company. An early assignment was the New Market whose walls cracked dangerously and had to be rebuilt, then a roof he was constructing at Boat Quay fell down and killed some workers, and the flag-staff on the grandly named Mount Faber, being inadequately conducted, was within a month struck by lightening and destroyed. The Grand Jury then complained that two little bridges he had constructed across the Canal were, by their flatness, obstructing boats at high tide so that their centres should be raised. But the Major, no doubt believing that even the sea would bow to the demands of a servant of the Honourable Company, said that instead he would dredge the Canal to lower the water level!

One of Coleman's finest and most useful buildings is the Institution. This lies at the north end of the Plain and is the best school we have though that, if truth be told, is no high praise. Education does not appear to rank high in the priorities of Europeans here. Their own children will be sent home for schooling and they seem careless of the education of others, leaving it to the missions. The Institution is an imposing building, as Raffles wished it to be, and has some 130 boys at present, with a small school for girls, most classes being taught in English though a few in Chinese. Then there is Keasbury's School which welcomes all comers, and the Roman Catholics have close by their church a school for boys and now, from early this year, another for girls. Indeed the boys' school, still only a wooden building, is soon to be enlarged and rebuilt. And of course it must not be forgotten that those of the Celestial Kingdom greatly value learning and without doubt there must be much education going on in the Chinese quarters. One of these now warrants the name 'school'; Mr Tan Kim Seng, the father of our picnicking friend, has this year established a Free School in Amoy Street and a plaque there tells of his desire to 'transform this barren land into a place of the learned'. A most worthy and most

The Singapore Institution.

Chinese sentiment. As for the Malays, I am told that what learning they give their young in formal fashion is largely the learning by heart of the words of the Prophet.

As the Institution is under-used and conveniently situated, it also houses a public library and a museum. The library was started largely by our good Dr Little, who called for shareholders some ten years ago both to purchase and donate books. The museum was started somewhat later, again growing from donations, the latest being from the Governor who, with some fanfare, has this year donated a fine collection of local weapons and a nice portfolio of illustrations of natural history. Of other municipal endeavours, botanic gardens have twice been established and twice abandoned, and I hear of no plans to see if the third time would be luckier.

Pity your friend, Harry. I have today spent the most tedious time in the company of lawyers. We have had some indications that all is not well with our books from Penang and so Mr Carnie wished to consult Mr Logan, thinking it wise that I should act as scribe. Well, we started at half past nine and continued until five, breaking only for a lunch of such ample proportions that it was with the greatest difficulty that I did not slouch unconscious over the desk as the afternoon dragged on. So it is a pleasure tonight to complete this letter to you, to think of all the joys of living here, and to remember you and your family on this Christmas Eve.

With love and remembrances to all friends,

Ben

Wednesday, 10 January 1855

My dear Harry,

My first letter to you of a new year which I hope will bring much happiness to us, our families and our friends. Now, if I tell you that it did not start in the most auspicious way, do not take that as any prelude to future happenings. Can a New Year celebration with the Great and the Good be expected to be enjoyed? Yes, it can, but not in the circumstances under which I saw in 1855.

We had been asked to the event at the Church's house, and even my uncle, a man who enjoys a party, was none too enthusiastic but felt that there was no polite way in which to decline. Our departure from home was delayed by some mishap to the carriage, which I initially thought was misfortune as I remembered the excellent wedding held there some months ago. But later I saw it as one of the few pieces of luck that evening. We finally got to the place after nine to find the rooms already crowded and insufferably hot. Some effort had been made at decoration with flowers and greenery, but both were succumbing to the stagnant air and wilting as we watched. In one room a small band was playing badly and I enjoyed a waltz with Mary. She dances most beautifully even when with child and remains always cool under the most trying of circumstances, whereas the other women present were already bedraggled by the heat. Eventually a boy arrived at our side and smilingly presented us with glasses of a yellowish liquid which he informed us was 'orange wine'. A sip of this extraordinary drink proved all that was possible, even for those in urgent need of stimulation, so shortly at Mary's suggestion one of the wilting plants felt its benefits and we partook of the only other drink available – some tea whose preparation had clearly involved no more than the rinsing of a few leaves in copious amounts of tepid water.

At about half past 10 o'clock a general movement was made in the direction of the dining room downstairs and, as I was both hungry and thirsty, I let myself be swept along by the tide. But it soon became apparent to all that our hosts had grossly underestimated either the number of their guests or their capacity for food, but I did managed to obtain at least a snack before it all ran out and the tide which had flowed so hopefully to the supper table ebbed back upstairs again.

There I was circulating somewhat hesitantly, wondering whether I could get closer to the Misses Dyce, who are interestingly known as the Dicey Daughters, or whether politeness demanded that I spoke to our host's dull daughter, when an old gentleman sitting on an expansive sofa asked me if I would care to join him. This turned out to be Captain Scott, one of our oldest and most respected figures, a cousin of Sir Walter and son of one of the earliest settlers in Penang, he himself coming from there to Singapore in the very early days. He had for long been Harbour Master here and had just started to tell me of those days, the second piece of good fortune of the evening, when I was dragged away by our hostess.

Eventually the hands of the clock crept towards midnight and glasses were raised, toasts drunk and speeches made to usher in the new year. At last there seemed some genuine celebration, but it was with great relief that soon thereafter my uncle called us to our carriage which being one of the last to arrive was one of the first to depart, the third and final piece of luck of the evening. Once home, I gratefully removed my sodden clothes, washed myself down and then slept like a child.

The first day of the year, despite its inauspicious start, proved a day to be remembered, the whole town turning out for a splendid regatta and other sports, the harbour alive with racing boats, the Esplanade with a myriad of sporting competitions, and the whole seafront lined with families of all classes and colours. Sensibly, each community celebrates all European festivities as well as their own thus enjoying two New Years every twelve months.

One happy coincidence of that day was that I happened to be with my uncle when Mr Whampoa, one of our leading Chinamen, came by. My uncle knows him well, and in introducing me obtained an invitation for us to visit him at his home. Now, you may say that Whampoa is hardly a Chinese name and you would be right. His real name is Mr Hoo Ah Kay, but he is always called after his company which is called after his birth-place which is near Canton and which is named Whampoa! He apparently came here as a boy some 25 years ago to join his father's grocery business, and, having turned that into the main provisioner of ships in Singapore, has prospered exceedingly. Some years ago he bought a neglected nutmeg plantation north of the town, there built a house and has since turned the surroundings into the finest garden in the Settlement.

Thus a few days later in the cool of the morning, breakfast time being the accepted hour to visit a Chinese family, we found ourselves bowling along the Serangoon Road, Mr Whampoa's house lying about three miles from my uncle's. The garden is completely walled with a fine entrance gate between high posts elaborately ornamented with dragons. The house, set well back, is surprisingly unpretentious, a large two-storied place of simple design, the deep verandas hung with ornamental

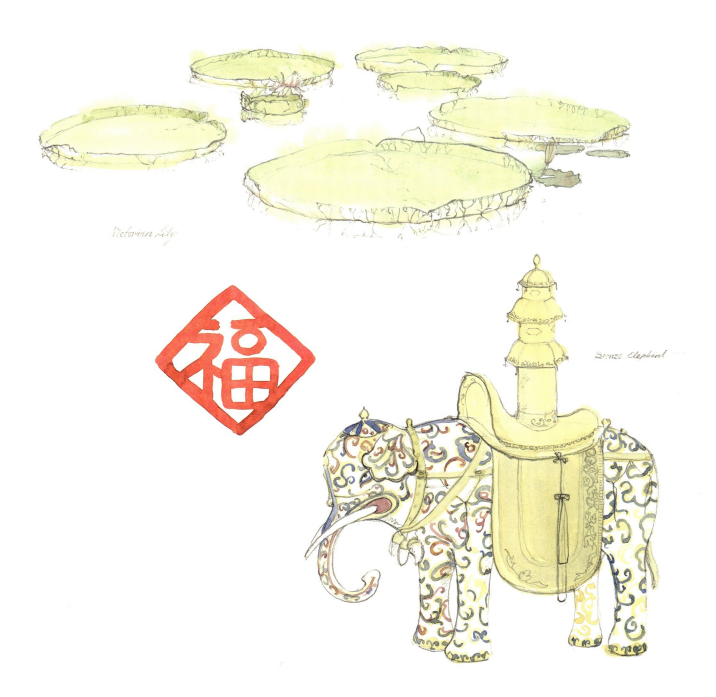

Victorian Lily

Bronze Elephant

bird-cages. A gardener hurried up and took our cards, posting them through a slot beside the finely carved front doors. Presently these were opened and we were ushered into a large cool hall to meet the owner. Mr Whampoa, coming down from the living rooms upstairs, greeted us most graciously and in impeccable English, and, after tea was served, as he and my uncle talked I took the opportunity to view both owner and room, both as elegant and sophisticated in their way as anything to be seen in the salons of London. The man is not tall but certainly good-looking, perhaps in his late thirties, and with a delightful twinkle in his eye. His queue, beautifully plaited with red silk thread, fell to his waist over a fine white calico jacket worn with spacious trousers of the same material. The room was stuffed with objects as in a museum, much of the furniture being of mahogany inlaid with mother-of-pearl and ivory and thus, though surprising to look at, of the most uncomfortable nature. In the centre stood a large table carrying a bronze elephant with a pagoda on its back, and nearby, suspended from two great elephant tusks, hung a huge gong about 4 feet in diameter inlaid with golden dragons. Against one wall rose a splendid altar of red lacquer at least a dozen feet high, the other walls being decorated with hangings of red silk with Chinese characters embroidered on them.

The garden must be of about a dozen acres, with straight paths and winding walks leading to arbours, tea houses, canals and ponds, all beautifully kept. A particular climbing shrub, apparently a sort of fig, had been trained on wires and clipped into crocodiles, dolphins, elephants and dragons with great staring eyes, so that in places it seemed almost like a frozen zoo. But flowers were abundant also, some in the soil, others hanging in baskets, and yet others growing out of the trees. These were mainly orchids and of such remarkable shapes and spectacular colours as to leave me open-mouthed. And in one of the ponds were quite the largest leaves I had ever seen, fully the size of opened umbrellas. This remarkable plant had apparently come as a present from the King of Siam. Nearby under a sheltering roof was a large tank containing fish of the brightest colours, sapphire, ruby, topaz and emerald, which rushed to the surface when Mr Whampoa tapped the glass and then followed his finger around the tank in a state of great excitement. Next was his particular favourite, a pet ape, and so to the aviary, deer pens and turtle pond. After taking further tea in the house we said our farewells, and I was back at my desk well before luncheon.

Another pleasure from such visits with my uncle is to find that, wherever we go, he is held in the highest esteem. The English, at least those I respect, clearly enjoy his company, value his fine tenor voice at parties, and appear often to seek his advice in private. More than once I have heard the story, told with much mirth, of his famous dinner for which he forgot to make arrangements, so in the morning sent his head boy round to the houses of his guests to discretely collect their own dinners, for which later he was profusely thanked. And he is also on intimate terms with many of the natives, be they wealthy merchants like Mr Whampoa or poor labourers, one day visiting the Sultan and the next taking tea with fishermen. His policing work requires that he goes about town at all hours of the

guppies

Whampoa's Moongate

topiary

day and night, so that we never know when he will be home. As he is a good listener and thoroughly trusted, people will confide in him knowing that he will not divulge the source of any information, and it seems that little goes on that he does not know about.

And he is blessed with a good wife. The more I get to know her the more I like Mary who is both quiet and humorous, a devoted mother and a merry companion. Although you could meet her likes in London, if you were lucky, yet she was born here of good mixed parentage and has never left the Settlement. Some thirty years ago Dr Jose d'Almeida, a surgeon on board a Portuguese man o' war sailing by found that he liked the island and, with a growing family which eventually reached 20 children, no longer fancied the itinerant life and so chose to settle. Thomas Crane arrived here that self-same year but quite by chance. Sailing for India he was shipwrecked off the coast of Spain but managed to swim to a deserted shore. Living off rats and shellfish for a month, he was almost despairing of life when rescued by a vessel bound for Singapore. There he decided to stay and within the year had founded a firm of auctioneers and married the eldest of the good Doctor's daughters. And in turn one of their many children, Mary, married Uncle Tom when she was but 16 and he twice her age. Mr Crane still lives nearby, having a fine house and coconut plantation at Geylang to the north.

Now, two months into the north-east monsoon, the harbour is crowded with junks from China, newly arrived. Why junks are so named I do not know for the Chinese do not call them thus, but junks they are to Englishmen. They are large vessels, perhaps of 800 tons, and filled with an amazing array of goods, the most valuable to the Settlement being people. To call men 'goods' might seem unkind, but goods these people are for they are bought – the 'sinkehs' about which I earlier told you. The junks are gaily painted, glittering with white and red and green and black, and on their bows two great big eyes. Miss Cooke told me that the Chinese believed that without its eyes a boat could not find its way back to China, but when I laughed about this to Lim he said, very seriously, no, they were not eyes – wooden eyes could not see – but they were charms to give the boat good luck. Grinning through the bows are two six-pounders, with five more along each side and a further two on the lofty stern. This heavy armament is ostensibly carried to deter pirates, whose depredations in the seas about here I have already mentioned, but in harbour its chief use seems to be to produce those stunning noises in which Chinamen delight. As the vessels are large, buyers of their goods are ferried out to them to view the pigs and tobacco, silks, sugars, teas and vegetables, crackers, joss-sticks, matches and candles, crockery, clothing and umbrellas, and as the bargaining gets under way the decks are as hectic and noisy as a market place.

Already the Chinese are preparing for their own new year which falls in the middle of next month. The shops are piling high spices and dried foods,

*Chinese Junk*

108

lanterns and paper hangings, tobacco and brandy, silk shirts and leather sandals. But what is this? Down the street I hear a commotion and in the distance see flags waving. In the midst of life, we are in death… it is a funeral, and the people on the street withdraw to the side to let it pass. They stand and stare but make no acknowledgement of its solemn nature. First comes a woman and two little children, the wife a Malay and dressed as for the market save for a black arm-band, the elder child a boy marching purposefully leading his sister by the hand. Then friends, members of the corpse's kongsi, and the band, some hammering away on gongs, others blowing manfully on reed instruments, their purpose apparently not to make music but rather the loudest of noises to scare evil away. The coffin, a great tree-trunk hollowed, is decked with banners and carried on the shoulders of a dozen men, and then come other mourners with bright umbrellas. The cemetery is on a hill-side, the graves shaped like the Greek omega, the head-stones fine granite, the inscriptions deeply cut and painted red and gold. Here a new pit has been dug where the father will be laid, the mourners scattering paper money over him to give him wealth in the hereafter. Only the children will be seen to shed tears today.

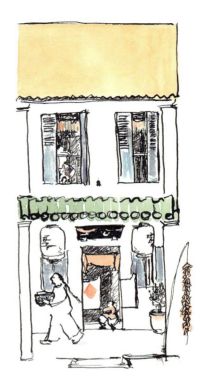

One pleasure we never had in London is hunting and I think that, Harry, you will enjoy it tremendously. Last Saturday I went out for such a trip with Bob Read and George Crane, my aunt's brother but little older than I. We started early from Boat Quay, sailing west on the morning breeze to the Jurong River, the three of us, two boatmen and Mustard, George's terrier. The Jurong is really little more than a creek, and turning into it we passed rapidly from the glare of the open sea through thin mangroves to the shade of thick jungle. Here the boatmen let us drift and we got a few shots at various birds but the trees were so dense that all I got were a couple of large pigeons. Bob was more fortunate and got one fine hornbill which luckily fell where it could be retrieved.

Monkeys and crocodiles were plentiful, but the latter were so wary that I had no more than a glimpse of them, a log-like back or a large splash from a mud-bank. These fearsome creatures are quite plentiful hereabouts and often seen in the rivers beyond Kampong Glam. Occasionally they will attack people who are bathing, and have been known to carry off not just children but even adults, but it is their depredations on fowl by the shore which riles the villagers. Of course it is for tigers that Singapore is more famous, and with good reason; not long ago it was said that they killed a man each

Mangrove swamp

day, and even now it is said that two a week are taken. Certainly at Bukit Timah my friends there have heard them roar a few times at dusk and they may come quite close to the town. George tells me that at Geylang where he lives, they can often be heard between 7 and 9 at night though he has seldom spotted one.

The most amusing animals hereabouts are the monkeys which can readily be seen in both forest and village. The Malays keep them as pets, using them to collect the nuts from the tall coconut palms, and it is an interesting occupation to watch one at work high up in the slender trees carefully choosing which nut to pick and let fall to his master below. Where we were they certainly were abundant, but although we hit four only one fell, landing on dry land on a sort of island in the river. George was determined to get it so that I could sample it for dinner, and sent Mustard after it, crocodiles or no. The dog floundered through water and mud to the monkey, whereupon a furious fight ensued. This made us all so excited that the two boatmen soon followed and managed eventually to reach the struggling creatures. The monkey was quickly dispatched and the dog retrieved, surprisingly unhurt despite the ferocity of the struggle. But let me tell you, it is no easy matter even for one as hungry as myself, to carve and devour a monkey, the shape not the taste being the sticking point.

Now I must finish in some haste to catch the mail. Today I have been delayed as I spent too long this afternoon at the horse auctions. These are held about once a month in Commercial Square, and are a fine cause of an afternoon for gathering and gossiping. The animals may just be being sold on but most are new arrivals, brought from Java and other parts of the Dutch Indies, the finest coming from Australia. So Klings are there bidding for nags for their gharries, towkays for steeds for their broughams, and the odd Englishman for a racer. It is all great fun.

In haste from your busy friend,

*Ben*

Bullock Cart

*Saturday, 20 January 1855*

Dear Harry,

I am delighted to receive your letter of the 6th of December last and to know that you are now definitely coming to join me here. Yes, Uncle can write a persuasive letter, as he did earlier to my own dear father, and I am most happy to know that he has now worked his magic on your's and that Mr Russell has blessed your journey. Yes, as my uncle wrote, he and my aunt insist that you stay with us until you find lodgings that suit you.

You said that you would be booking your passage this month so I much look forward to your next letter when you will, no doubt, tell me the date of your arrival. It is all most exciting.

I have also warned my friends about what is soon to descend upon them. Lim is, I think, already relishing the thought of introducing another ignorant barbarian to the subtleties of the Celestials, and Kim Cheak the chance of again winning at fives.

And I thank you for your birthday wishes; soon we will again be two years apart. Then but one more year until I am a man in law as well as looks and action!

Ah, the sights of Singapore, sights I will soon be enjoying in your company. Along the street at a decent clip comes an elegant phaeton, a handsome Chinaman lolling in the back on the way to his go-down. It pulls out to pass a buffalo cart, the buffaloes encased in mud, the creaking of its great wheels almost drowning out the harsh cries of the scrawny Kling who commands it. The Chinaman continues down the middle of the road, overtaking a gharry which is pulling into Boustead & Company's offices. And who should alight but the lovely Miss Oxley who, if one was seeking a wife to enhance one's status, would be one of the few here who would be eligible. Sadly, her good looks and fine manners are not matched either by her intelligence or humour as I found one evening when closeted with her after an excellent dinner. Indeed, I remember the food better than our conversation. But

Traveller's Palm

wait, what is this? A most startling conveyance, an old-fashioned sort of victoria powered by a pair of piebalds of rather unequal size, heaves into view with a high leather front on the top of which the driver perches. Deep in the body of the chariot sits the owner, diminutive in height but thick set, his face largely hidden by a tall black silk hat set well down. At the back on the foot-board, towering over all, stands a very large and very black man, holding elegantly in his hand a horse-fly brush.

Now it comes to my mind that this could be Captain Cloughton about whom I have heard some interesting stories. Although only recently arrived to take charge of building the dry dock at New Harbour, he has already caused consternation amongst polite society. Assuming him to be in town to visit some office or shop, I quicken my pace, or more truthfully run pell-mell when I can, to see if I can get a better view when he alights. This I achieve and the reward is ample. Below the tall hat his clean shaven face is set off by a spotless white shirt with turned-down collar and black silk bow. There is no waistcoat below the straight-cut coat of naval blue, this leading down to the whitest of duck trousers and the shiniest pair of patent leather shoes. There is not long to relish the spectacle before he shouts instructions to his men and rapidly disappears into John Little's emporium.

Later enquiry revealed that this was indeed the Captain and his African factotum Babu, once his bosun. His problem seems to be that what elegance he aspires to in dress he loses in language. He has, apparently, frequently been heard, even in the presence of ladies, berating his servants most fiercely; and sometimes he will, in front of others and for no very obvious reason, reach up and give Babu a good slap, which the black man takes without demure. But master and servant are obviously very close. Once when asked to dine out he replied "What's the use? Far better to chance Babu's concoction at home. It will be just as good." Thus now the Captain is seldom seen gracing the tables of the best society.

Our own all too modest celebrations for the new year now well behind us, those for the Chinese are gathering pace. On the 17th of next month their Tiger year gives way to the Rabbit. Quite why the years are animals I do not know, but animals they are, and twelve in all. And speaking of tigers, and before their year is out, I have at last set eyes on one! Not alive, I am happy to say, but dead, though fearsome even in death. A few years ago the Government ordered pits and traps to be set, but the first creature caught in a pit was a Malay hunter, horribly impaled on the spikes at the bottom, and thereafter these were well marked. The Government gives a reward of $50 for each tiger killed, and the merchants' club adds a similar amount. Thus it was that I saw my beast borne in a procession to the Government office to collect the reward, not lying as if it had been shot, which was the truth, but propped up by bamboo in a standing position, the mouth open and the tail erect!

*Telok Ayer Market*

Now do not think that a mere hundred dollars is the full worth of these beasts. Every part has an additional value. The skin is carefully removed, dried and sold to a European for a rug. The Sultan claims the liver, which when dried and powdered into medicine is worth twice its weight in gold. The gall is also highly prized, and Chinamen dry the blood and boil the bones to make valuable tonics. The eyes, which are of great size, seem particularly precious for the lens is a valuable charm and will be set in gold as a ring. The flesh is perhaps no more than food; we ourselves were later served it as a stew, but it seemed to me tough and unpalatable, so perhaps it too has redeeming magical properties.

As the Chinese new year approaches, so the shops get even fuller and the streets ever more crowded. Of course shop and street are here both market-places, the covered ways and the warmth of the climate making outdoor selling much more conducive than on the streets of London. But we also have two true markets, both of course wonderfully full of life and, I suppose, of death. On the river there is New Market, correctly Ellenborough Market, but my favourite is the old one, down by the sea not far from the fort, Telok Ayer Market, mostly housed in a fine octagonal building, again by our friend Coleman. The din is tremendous, salesmen shouting, buyers bargaining at the tops of their voices, and all amidst the grunts, quacks, cackles and cries of the animals soon to be turned into juicy pigs' heads, flattened ducks no more than an inch thick, and large bowls of chickens' feet.

Of course there is stall upon stall of fruits and vegetables, so varied, abundant and colourful. Yes, there are things you will recognise - beans, radishes, cabbages, onions, and even apples and oranges from over the seas. But also sweet potatoes which are not potatoes, egg-plants that do not bear eggs,

116

chillies that are very hot. And yams, melons, bananas, cucumbers, durian, mangosteen, pineapple, papaya – all names you will have to conjure with until you arrive. But my favourite area is the poultry market. On account of the heat everything arrives alive, in baskets, cages or coops, or just tied by the feet and thrown down anyhow, and the crowing, quacking, cooing and gobbling are really marvelous. As well as the usual chickens and ducks, there are colourful pheasants and jungle fowl, plump pigeons and quail, brilliant parrots and lories, and even a talking mynah, like a colourful starling. On my first visit I let myself purchase a cage of tiny parrots no bigger than bullfinches and of lovely colour. And having made one purchase everyone seemed to think that I wanted a multitude of birds, and soon I was surrounded by an enthusiastic throng all with parrots in their hands or on their shoulders.

Another place of marvels is not within the octagon but in a neighbouring building built out over the sea, the tides keeping it quite the sweetest smelling fish market you can imagine. From it two jetties run out to sea so boats can tie up just a few yards from where their catches are sold. And what catches – alive and swimming in buckets, struggling for life in bundles laid on slabs, or expired and gutted and filleted: crabs like enormous spiders, buckets of little shells, heaps of oysters, woven baskets of tiny dried fish, octopus flattened like shoe leather (and in fact of similar taste), pink shrimps, blue fishes, red lobsters and black sea slugs like sausages, called delightfully, and no doubt accurately, by the locals 'butoh keling' or Indian prick.

Lim has been a wonderful fount of knowledge as we approach the celebrations, he and his family delighting to educate me in Chinese ways. Sadly, he is the only one who can speak English but all have been most kind, and the lovely Mey Lin is always a pleasure to accompany. Between them, and without being the least aware of it, they have loaded me with more gifts than I will ever be able to repay in kind.

At this time the Chinese theatre becomes ever more popular, and one evening last week the Lims took me past one, believing that a mere glimpse of this entertainment would suffice for a boy from London. The stage raised on poles had been set up in a clearing between some houses and was decorated most gorgeously. Upon it to one side were about a dozen musicians and in the centre a number of characters disporting themselves, each as gaily decorated as the stage and each bursting into song or chant at odd intervals accompanied by wailing violins, clashing gongs and pounding drums. At other times they turned their hand to mime or to most athletic acrobatics. Sometimes the action was pure drama with swords and manly confrontations, sometimes as indecent as one could hope to see in public with confrontations of an altogether more intimate nature. Of course I could not follow the plot, if plot there was, but at least I could tell the heroes by their white faces, the fools by their red noses, and the ladies by their sumptuous apparel, the latter being essential as all are in fact men.

At dramatic or indecent moments the audience hushed or cheered loudly, but in all other ways they showed no discipline whatsoever, wandering around smoking and talking to each other as attendants with food and drinks passed amongst them. Some even climbed the stairs to the stage and sat there, their legs dangling over the edge while children played around them, none of this appearing to distract the actors from their play. This single-mindedness was certainly needed for Mr Lim told me that the play had been going on for three days and had another two to run.

Whereas the Chinese are well provided with theatre, their requirements being simple, the Europeans now have nowhere for any public function, strange in a place with the pretensions of Singapore. The Assembly Rooms at the foot of the Hill were quite suitable, with a decent portico in the centre and a hall to the left for dinners and to the right for theatricals, the grandly named "Theatre Royal", but it was built some time ago, and being of lathe and plaster with an atap roof is now dilapidated. However it is about to be given a new lease of life, for in March we will welcome Catherine Hayes all the way from London to regale us with her songs. A visit from such a celebrity is unheard of, and the worthies have seen the necessity of doing something about the Rooms. But the gossip is that at three dollars a seat, even such a singer may fail to attract the masses. The renovation of the Rooms has in turn revived the fortunes of the Dramatic Club, long defunct, who now threaten to amuse us with their dramas.

Surrounding the town are large plantations, some owned by Europeans, others by Chinese and most with spacious bungalows in their midst. To the north coconuts seem favoured, and at Geylang my aunt's family, the Cranes, have many acres. To the west where the land is more hilly it seems to be nutmeg country. You may think, with a climate that is always warm and wet and seeing the forest is so fine, that all would grow here with the greatest facility but plantation life has surprised many by its difficulty. Cloves, cotton, sago and sugar have all proved unsuccessful, and now the lovely nutmeg trees are suffering from some fell disease which may spell the end of this valuable crop. It is in fact the Chinese and not the Europeans who seem better suited to plantation work. Although their gambier trees are apparently not flourishing, these are being rapidly replaced by pineapple, and pepper seems to thrive under their ministrations.

Last week we had a most jolly visit to one of these plantations, to a family called the Kerrs, he yet another of the Scots and she a Malay. Mr Kerr has built a house on top of a small hill, Bukit Chermin or Glass Hill, which overlooks the western entrance to New Harbour. From the verandah you can look down a hundred feet or so to the sea which lies like a sheet of glass below. To the left lies Pulau Hantu, Ghost Island, and behind it a low hill, on one of whose tops stands a solitary palm like a weird sentinel. To the right the view is even wider, looking westwards out to sea where distant flashes of lightening reveal more clearly where sky and sea meet. The house, like many of those built in the

Chinese Opera

— View from Bukit Chermin of Western Harbour.

country, is most spacious with the dining room below convenient for the kitchen, and the sitting room on the first floor opening on to a wide balcony over the carriage porch. Such ample accommodation is clearly needed for the place is filled with children of all ages, most from their colour clearly belonging to the master of the house but others all the shades of the East.

Lunch was taken on the veranda, with a fine view of the sea and cooled by a very pleasant breeze which gently rustled the surrounding palm trees. Grilled fowl, ham and sweet potatoes, wine and pale ale were first set before us, then a variety of sweetmeats and when these were devoured cheese followed. And finally came the height of the banquet, a huge platter heaped with fruit, pomeloes, oranges, bananas, pineapple and, on a separate dish, durian. Would this suffice do you think, Harry?

The durian? No, I cannot describe this object to you, Harry. Indeed, it is indescribable. Better for you to wait with bated breath to discover it for yourself.

Now, on this enticing note I must end, but before I do so can I beg you to bring the largest quantity of books that you can manage. Beg, borrow or steal enough to fill a large trunk. Yes, there is a library here but I fear that the donors of books often donate only the most turgid and unreadable. I have asked my father to give you some to bring, but you know my taste better than he and could, I am sure, pack things for your friend that he might not deem suitable for a son.

Looking forward so much to learning of the dates of your voyage, I remain ever your good friend,

*Ben*

*Thursday, 15 March 1855*

My dear Harry,

Your letter of the 20th of January is to hand with the dates of your voyage. How glad I am! At last there is no need to attempt to persuade you of the wisdom of such action. Rather, I can now wish you the safest of voyages with the fairest of winds, and say how much I look forward to the 15th of June.

Our partying continues. Firstly for the arrival of a new cousin; little William was born on the 11th of last month, Mary accomplishing the task with her usual calmness and good sense. By the time you arrive he will, with good fortune, have decided that there is no longer need to demonstrate to one and all, and always in the depths of the night, the remarkable capacity of his lungs. And then we have enjoyed New Year for the Chinese, my own fine birthday, and grandest of all – a ball to celebrate the founding of Singapore 36 years ago. On the 6th of last month we repaired to the rejuvenated Assembly Rooms, and everybody who was anybody, and even some of us considered nobody, was there. The place was wonderfully transformed with the flags of all the nations visiting the port decorating the walls, and garlands of vegetation and flowers hanging everywhere, still unwilted. The Governor started the dancing with a quadrille and the swirling colours were magnificent; European officers in their smartest uniforms, the rich clothes of a Malay prince, the brilliant colours of the Siamese chiefs, the flowing robes of the Arabs, the sober costumes of the rich Chinese, the sparkling vestments of the Armenian merchants. And then of course some really nice girls, of every shade from brown Malay to pale European. Old Jerry Kulkeus, a gentleman of Dutch descent, was there with his niece, a pretty slightly brown girl with the most lovely eyes of soft dark blue and the most elegant figure. I danced with her as often as I could, and she, like most Indian girls, never seemed to feel the heat whilst I was melting.

For our good Governor, the famous Butterpot, this was the last such ball he would attend for he leaves us to retire to England at the end of the month. News had recently arrived of his elevation to the rank of Major-General and this was the first opportunity for many to congratulate him. He has recently donated a fine portrait of Sir James Brooke to the Library, the Rajah being a most generous donor to that institution, and this was hung at the ball for all to admire. It is rumoured that this donation was not entirely selfless, for it is said that the Governor has for long been desirous of getting a portrait of himself installed in the Settlement before his departure, and this he has now achieved. Just before midnight the band grew silent, and Butterpot was asked to reveal his picture to us all. Full length it is, a regal pose with medals, swords and plumes aplenty. And well received, for most have a soft spot for him.

And then to supper, another splendid feast, the *pièce de résistance* of which was a huge pie placed on the high table. When the crust was ceremonially broken, out flew a couple of dozen small birds, all about the table and into the faces and the laps of the assembled company, much to everyone's amusement. After order was restored, the Governor proposed toasts to the Queen and to the memory of Raffles, and then the dancing commenced again and did not let up until 5 in the morning.

Celebrations continued a few days later with the ushering in of the Year of the Rabbit by the Chinese, celebrations more colourful and more noisy than anything the English could manage, and more prolonged. At their quietest I find the Chinese a hectic people and here is their grandest festival! Weeks before, the markets began to fill with an even richer variety of food, ever more colourful lanterns and banners began to appear on house and temple, and the streets became even more thronged with eager purchasers and desperate gamblers. To enter the new year in good grace it is necessary to finish the business of the old, to settle all accounts and tidy home and shop, to drive from them evil spirits with the explosion of string upon string of fire-crackers, and of course to feast as if famine loomed. The evening before is a family affair, but on the day itself I took the opportunity to visit my friends, the Lims and the Ang brothers, and was already by luncheon filled to the scuppers with Chinese delicacies.

By the way, your place on the cricket team has already been reserved! This I ensured after the game last Sunday when Abu Bakar asked me to Kampong Glam to meet his father. His family are feeling well pleased as on the Saturday before there was some sort of treaty concluded which apparently means Abu will eventually become Sultan. The whole thing is not easy to unravel; while Abu's father is not Sultan (his title is Temenggong of Johore), he has all the power and the ear of the Governor; and the Sultan of Johore has but the title and no power! Anyway, Abu tells me that Sultan, Temenggong, Malays and even the British are happy with this conclusion.

The Temenggong is a stately man, not short and dark but tall and quite fair as he is, I am told, more Arab than Malay. His father was, as it were, pensioned off by Raffles, so they are well provided

Malay Prince

Arab

Chinese

*Istana at Kampong Glam*

for and their house is a fine one. There in a large room I was granted an audience. And 'audience' it was, blessedly brief, my visit really being so that Abu could show me a little of his home.

Last Sunday we welcomed another newcomer to our team, one whom I am sure you will find amusing – why, he is almost as confident of himself as you and but a couple of years younger! George Dare may belie his name in looks, tall and thin with large spectacles, rather scholarly, but his life and present disposition well suit it. His family now resides beside the Dunmans on Beach Road and within the day I had heard George's life story and more. I fear his adventures make my life seem most constrained. They certainly started early as he was born at sea, his father a captain whom his mother in her young days always followed. He arrived in Singapore first in 1841 at the tender age of one and, as he was about to be joined by a younger brother, he and his mother remained when his father sailed for China. At the end of the year mother and boys sailed also for China, only to be wrecked on the first day of the new year. There followed a couple of days in the boats until a pirate prahu came upon the little flotilla and they were taken captive. Some of the crew apparently suffered badly but the women and children were quite well treated. Two boats were taken in tow, the others destroyed, and when one night they were near to a shore, the rope was cut and they made their escape. George had surprised everyone by his liveliness throughout this ordeal, but he had by chance discovered some bananas left below a sail at the bottom of the boat and had secretly devoured them all.

Eventually mother, George and John again reached Singapore and next time sailed without mishap to join their father. At the age of five George was sent with his brother to England for an education, according to George more to relieve his parents of their encumbrance than through concern for learning. Anyway, the Dares have now settled here and so the boys have come to join them. As yet I have not met John as he has been ill, but of George I could already tell you more. But I will desist as you will soon be meeting him and will I know hear all that I have heard.

A week or two ago, indeed the very night before my birthday, we had one of those strange evenings that perhaps only Singapore can provide. My uncle and aunt were entertaining the McDougalls, Mr McDougall leading the mission in Sarawak and returning there via Singapore with his entourage after a period of leave in England. The Reverend is himself an ebullient and loud fellow and his wife of surprising humour and grace, so I was enjoying the occasion much more than I had feared. Just as the meat was being served a most dreadful storm blew up, vivid lightening illuminating us at the very instant the house shook with thunderous explosions, the wind blowing the hanging tatties out from the windows and taking the napkins from our knees. Soon the worst seemed over and, after the servants had restored some order to the table, we continued our meal. But we had hardly finished the meat when a servant spoke urgently to my uncle and then brought in a white faced and panting Malay. Apparently lightening had hit a house in Kampong Malacca, killing four young boys sleeping side by side but leaving unharmed their mother lying next to them! This dreadful story caused great consternation, and my uncle and Mr McDougall left for the kampong to see what help could be rendered and the evening came to a sorry end.

Here I am, meandering on mindless of the fact that you will soon be here to share it all with me. Before you leave, please be so good as to visit my family again. They will as always enjoy your company, and then you can tell me at first hand exactly how they fare. And now, let me refer again to my sentiments expressed at the start of this letter, and assure you that your decision to come here will never be regretted and that I wait with excitement your arrival and our reunion.

This is the last letter you will receive from me before you leave London. Wishing you God speed on your voyage, I remain, my dear Harry, ever your good friend,

*Ben*

# Dramatis Personae

*Fictional characters are marked with an asterisk.*

**Abu Bakar** [1835 - 1896]. Eldest son of Temenggong Daing Ibrahim [1811-1862], Rajah of Johore and *de facto* leader of the Singapore Malays. An astute businessman, Ibrahim grew wealthy, with a fine house at Telok Blangah. By the treaty of 10 March 1855 the powers of the Sultan of the old Johore-Riau Empire were invested in him, so that at his death Abu Bakar became Sultan of Johore.

**Allen, Charles Martin** [1839 - 1892]. Assistant to A.R. Wallace [q.v.] in the Malay Archipelago for four years, April 1854 – January 1856 and January 1860 – January 1862. Born in London, in 1862 he settled in Singapore where he married and raised a family of nine children, and where he died.

**Allen, Dr Henry A.** [died 1869]. Partner of Dr Robert Little [q.v.]

**Ang Kim Cheak** [1827 - 1870]. His father Ang Choon Seng [1805 - 1852] was born in Malacca but came to Singapore as a young man and established a commission agent and provisioning firm in Philip Street, 'Chin Seng'. After his death Kim Cheak, his eldest son, continued the business, later joined by his younger brother Kim Tee [1839 - 1901].

**Brooke, Sir James** [1803 - 1868]. First of the White Rajahs of Sarawak, Borneo. Born in India, he first visited Singapore in June 1839 and Sarawak two months later, being made Rajah in 1841. He was one of the heroes of early Victorian Britain, and was invested KCB in Singapore in 1848.

**Butterworth, The Hon. Colonel William George** [1800 - 1856]. Fifth Governor of the Straits Settlements, 1843 – 1855, for the Honourable East India Company [HEIC].

**Carnie, Charles** [born 1809/10]. One of many prominent Scots, he arrived in Singapore in the early 1830s, initially living with 'Louisa, a native woman', but in 1839 marrying Frances Amelia aged 16. He first became a partner in the trading firm Paterson & Co, and in 1842 moved to Martin, Dyce & Co. He built a house for himself at Cairnhill in 1840.

**Church, Thomas.** Resident Councillor, 1837 - 1856.

**Cloughton, Captain William** [born 1811]. As captain of a trading vessel he saw the need for a dry dock in Singapore, so settled there in 1854 and built one with his own and friends' investments.

**Coleman, George Drumgoole** [1795 - 1844]. The finest architect of early Singapore. Born in Ireland, he went first to Calcutta in 1815 and then to Batavia in 1820. He occasionally worked in Singapore 1822 – 1826 and settled there as surveyor, planner and architect 1826 – 1841. He left for London in July 1841, married in September 1842 and returned to Singapore in November 1843 where he died in March the following year.

**\*Cook, Benjamin.** The author of these letters, born in London 6 March 1835, the second of five children. His father was in business. His mother, who died in 1842, was the sister of Thomas Dunman [q.v.]. Later a partner in Russell & Cook on North Boat Quay, provisioning merchants.

**Cooke, Miss Sophia** [died 1895]. Arrived from England in 1853 to take over from Miss Grant the charge of the Chinese Girls' School, then with 20 girls, situated in Beach Road by the Mission Chapel. She became widely known in Singapore, for over forty years ministering to many, from homeless Chinese to members of the European police force.

**Crane, Thomas Owen** [ca 1800 - 1867]. Arriving in Singapore in 1825, the following year he married the eldest daughter of Dr Jose d'Almeida [q.v.]. Amongst their 14 children were **Mary**, later Mary Dunman [q.v.], and **George**. Their youngest child, Emilie Charlotte, was born on 20 April 1854, two days after Ben Cook arrived in Singapore. Founded the auctioneers and land agents Thomas O. Crane which in 1855 he handed over to his two eldest sons, the firm becoming Crane Brothers. He had a large house and coconut plantation at Geylang.

**D'Almeida, Dr Jose** [ ca 1780 – 1850]. In 1825, as a surgeon on a Portuguese warship sailing from Macau, he called at Singapore and decided to settle there. He had 19 or 20 children, his eldest daughter marrying Thomas Crane [q.v.] in 1826.

**Dare, George Mildmay.** Born in 1840, he first visited Singapore in 1841. He was sent to England for schooling in 1845, rejoining his parents in their house on the corner of Beach Road and Bras Basah Road in March 1855. He later joined Syme & Company's office for five years.

**De Sousa, Tertullian.** He and his brother Manuel were partners in the firm Aitken De Souza & Company.

**Devereux, The Hon. Humphry Bohun.** From the Indian Civil Service, he was one of two Commissioners at the inquiry into the actions of Sir James Brooke in 1854.

**Dunman, Thomas** [1815 – 1887]. Arriving in Singapore in 1842, he first worked for Martin, Dyce & Co. In September 1843 he joined the police service as Deputy Magistrate and Superintendent of Police under the Resident Councillor, Thomas Church [q.v.], and in 1857 was appointed the first independent Commissioner of Police. He retired in 1871 and returned to England four years later. On 4 January 1847 he married **Mary Anne Esther Crane** [born 1830], the 16-year-old daughter of Thomas Crane, by whom he had nine children between 1847 and 1861, the sixth, William, being born on 11 February 1855. He was described as "a man of great delicacy of feeling, benevolently dispositioned, high social powers, a fine singer, jolly companion, and a universal favourite".

**Dutronquoy, Gaston.** A Frenchman from Jersey, he arrived from France in 1839, starting the London Hotel and the Theatre Royal. He later disappeared near Muar, Johore, perhaps murdered.

**Dyce, Charles Alexander.** Coming from India in 1842, he became assistant in Martin, Dyce & Co. and the first secretary of the Singapore Sports Club. Keen on theatricals and a good water-colourist, he later became High Sheriff of the Straits Settlements.

**Faber, Major.** Arrived from Madras in September 1844 as the Superintending Engineer for the HEIC.

**Grant, Charles** [1831 – 1891]. Born at Kilgraston in Perthshire, Scotland, he joined the Navy at the age of 13. In 1845 he met Sir James Brooke in Sarawak who was greatly impressed by him, and in 1848 left the Navy to join Sir James as his Private Secretary. He worked in various posts in the government of Sarawak until 1861 when he returned to Scotland.

**Keasbury, Benjamin** [1811 – 1875]. Born in India, the son of a colonel in the Indian Army. In the 1830s he worked in Singapore, Batavia and America where he married. In 1837 he returned to Singapore to work as a missionary amongst the Malays, and thereafter never left the Settlement. In 1840 he opened a small school and in 1843 a new church on Prinsep Street, the Malay Chapel. In September 1846 as a widower he married Elizabeth Louisa Scott, less than 16 years old, daughter of Robert Scott.

**Kerr, Alexander John.** Registrar of the Singapore Court 1838 – 1855, much respected though not a professional lawyer.

**Light, Francis** [1740 – 1794]. Born in Suffolk, England, he joined the Navy and the Army before becoming a merchant associate with the HEIC. In 1786 he settled Penang Island on behalf of the Company.

**\*Lim Wee Cheng.** Born in Singapore in 1832, he was educated at the Anglo-Chinese College, Malacca, and later employed, with Ben Cook, as a clerk by Martin, Dyce & Co. He lived on the corner of Cross Street and South Bridge Road where his family had a general store.

**Little, Dr Robert** [born before 1820, died 1888]. Son of an Edinburgh lawyer and graduate of the university there, he arrived in Singapore in August 1840. He founded the Singapore Dispensary in Commercial Square where he lived, practising there with **Dr Henry Allen** [q.v.]. In 1844 he helped establish a library, in 1848 became Coroner, and in 1851 opened a private hospital for seamen. In 1882 he returned to Britain. His younger brother, **John**, with Cursetjee Frommurzee founded the merchants Messrs Little, Cursetjee & Co. in 1845, and when that partnership dissolved in 1853 with his brother **Matthew** established John Little & Company.

**Logan, Abraham** [born 1816]. Born in Berwickshire, he and his younger brother James [born 1819] moved to Penang in 1839 and to Singapore in 1842 to start a Law practice. He lived at Mount Pleasant off Thomson Road, with an office in Battery Road.

**McDougall, Rev. Frank** [1817 - 1886]. As a qualified doctor, he went as the first English missionary to Sarawak in 1848, remaining there with his wife **Harriette** [1818 – 1886] for 20 years. He was consecrated the first Bishop of Labuan & Sarawak in 1855.

**Marryat, Florence.** Daughter of Captain Marryat, a naval captain and well known Victorian novelist, particularly for *Masterman Ready*. Florence, also a novelist, married the son of Thomas Church in Singapore in September 1854.

**Maudit, Father A.** [died 1858]. A Frenchman who had worked in China, he was a Roman Catholic missionary in Singapore 1844 – 1858. In 1846 he founded St Joseph's Church at Bukit Timah as a plank and atap chapel, rebuilding it in stone in 1852 – 1853.

**Napier, William** [born 1804]. Son of a Professor of Law at Edinburgh University, in 1833 he became the first law Agent admitted in Singapore. In 1835 he founded the *Singapore Free Press* which he edited until 1846. In October 1844 he married George Coleman's widow [q.v.], his second wife, and adopted Coleman's infant son. In 1845 he became the first Freemason to be initiated in Singapore. A great friend of Sir James Brooke, he was Lieutenant Governor of Labuan Island off Borneo 1847 – 1851. In 1854 he built a house along Napier Road. His eldest brother David [born 1798] was a partner in the firm Napier & Scott, one of the first merchants in Singapore.

**Prinsep, Charles Robert.** Barrister at Law, Advocate-General of Bengal. The senior Commissioner at the inquiry into the actions of Sir James Brooke in 1854. Almost in his dotage, he suffered from a 'mental malady' to which he succumbed soon after.

**Raffles, Sir Thomas Stamford** [1781 – 1826]. Born to a seafaring father, he entered the service of the HEIC at the age of 14 and rose within 10 years to become Assistant Secretary of Penang [1805] and then Lieutenant-Governor of Java [1811]. Knighted in 1817, he founded Singapore in 1819, dying seven years later in England. Self-taught and extremely hard-working, he liked the peoples of the East and treated them with respect. According to Munsyi Abdullah 'he spoke in smiles'.

**Read, William Henry Macleod, 'WH'** [1819 – 1909]. Although born in London, his father at that time worked in Bencoolen, Sumatra, leaving there for Singapore in 1822 where he became a partner in A. L. Johnstone & Co. His mother and sister went to Singapore in 1824 but WH not until 1841, the following January replacing his father at Johnstone's. The Reads lived on Battery Road in the first house on entering the river, close by Johnstone's offices. In 1845 he became the second Mason to be initiated into the new lodge. He retired to Britain in 1887. His cousin, **Robert Barclay Read** [born 1828], arrived in Singapore in 1848.

**\*Russell, Harry.** The recipient of these letters, born in London 10 October 1836. His father was a merchant and he a clerk in a trading company. The youngest of a family of four, the eldest brother George [27] in the Army, Helen [24] and William [22]. He left London for Singapore on 8 May 1855, arriving there on 15 June. Later a partner in Russell & Cook on North Boat Quay, provisioning merchants.

**Scott, Captain William** [1778 – 1861]. Cousin of the novelist Sir Walter Scott [1771-1832] and son of James Scott [died 1810], a close associate of Francis Light [q.v.] and one of the first settlers in Penang. Harbour Master and Port Master of Singapore until about 1843, he lived at Hurricane House on the Claymore Estate, the third largest plantation on the island.

**Solomon, Abraham** [1798 - 1884]. Born in Baghdad, he arrived in Singapore about 1836. A leader of the small Jewish community, he had a shop and house on Boat Quay.

**Song Hoot Kiam** [1830 - 1900] Born in Malacca, the second of three sons of Song Eng Chong also born in Malacca [1799]. At 11 he went as a boarder to the Anglo-Chinese College, Malacca, whose principal, the Rev James Legge, took him and two other pupils to school in Huntly, Scotland, in 1846. There he remained for two years and was baptised. He settled in Singapore in late 1849 and soon thereafter married his first wife, Yeo Choon Neo. As one of the first Chinese Protestants in Singapore, he was closely involved in Keasbury's church of which he became treasurer. In 1853 he joined the Singapore office of the P & O and worked as the cashier there until retirement in 1895.

**Tan Kim Seng** [1805 - 1864]. Born in Malacca, he opened a trading house on Boat Quay, Kim-Seng & Co., before 1840. Appointed a JP in 1850, he was by then one of the most prominent of the Chinese in the Settlement. In 1849 he set up a school in Thian Hock Keng temple with Seah Eu Chin [1805 – 1883], and in 1854 built and endowed the Chinese Free School in Amoy Street. His son, **Tan Beng Swee** [1828 – 1884], born in Singapore, was made partner in his father's firm in 1852.

**Tan Tock Seng** [1798 – 1850]. Born in Malacca, he came to Singapore shortly after its founding. One of the richest of the early towkays, he financed in 1844 the building of the Chinese or Paupers' Hospital, and he was the first Chinese JP. On his death, the eldest of his three sons, **Tan Kim Ching** [1829-1892] took over the business; from 1851 to 1859 'Tan Kim-ching' was located on Boat Quay. In 1854 Kim Ching gave $3000 for the expansion of his father's hospital.

**Vaughan, Jonas Daniel** [1825 – 1891]. Born in England, he first saw Singapore as a midshipman in 1842 on his way to the first Opium War. In the late 1840s he was appointed First Officer on the HEIC steamer *Hooghly* in Singapore, in 1851 Superintendent of Police in Penang, in 1856 Master Attendant in Singapore, and in 1861 Police Magistrate. In 1869 while on leave in England he qualified as a barrister of the Middle Temple, and set up as an advocate and solicitor. In 1891 he was lost overboard from s.s. *Malacca* while returning from a visit to one of his married daughters at Alor Gajah, Malacca.

**Wallace, Alfred Russel** [1823 – 1913]. The great English naturalist, co-discoverer with Charles Darwin of the theory of evolution by natural selection. He spent eight years in the Malay Archipelago, 1854 – 1862, 'the central and controlling incident' of his life. He arrived in Singapore on 18 April 1854 with his assistant Charles Allen [q.v.], collecting there and around Malacca, and left for Sarawak on 16 October that year, returning for some months in early 1856 and again in early 1862 on his way back to England.

**Wan Eng Kiat** [1834 – 1919]. Born in Malacca, he came to Singapore in 1851, working first as a watchmaker, then entering the service of Martin, Dyce & Company.

**Whampoa [Hoo Ah Kay]** [1816 – 1880]. He arrived in Singapore from Whampoa near Canton in 1830 to join his father's provisioners in Telok Ayer Street. He rapidly became one of the Settlement's richest and most prominent citizens, admired by all sections of society. In 1869 he was appointed a member of the Legislative Council and an Extraordinary Member of the Executive Council, and was honoured by Queen Victoria in 1876.

**Woods, Robert Carr** [1816 – 1875]. Born in England, he travelled to Bombay in 1840, and then in 1845 to Singapore as first editor of the *Straits Times* which he later bought. Although not a professional lawyer, he was admitted Law Agent in 1849. Generally admired, the one blot on his reputation was his conduct over the 1854 Commission of Inquiry into the activities of Sir James Brooke.

**Wright, Captain George Tod.** Captain of the HEIC steamer *Hooghly*. He married a daughter of E. A. Blundell, sixth Governor of the Straits Settlements, 1855-1861.

# References

Bastin, J., 1994. *Travellers' Singapore, an anthology*. Oxford University Press, Kuala Lumpur.

Buckley, C.B., 1902. *An anecdotal history of old times in Singapore (1819-1867)*. 2 vols. Reprinted 1965, University of Malay Press, Kuala Lumpur.

Edwards, N., 1990. *The Singapore house and residential life 1819 – 1939*. Oxford University Press, Singapore.

Hancock, T. H. H., 1986. *Coleman's Singapore*. Malaysian Branch of the Royal Asiatic Society and Times Bookshop, Kuala Lumpur.

Jayapal, M., 1992. *Old Singapore*. Oxford University Press, Kuala Lumpur.

Lee Geok Boi, 2002. *The religious monuments of Singapore; faiths of our forefathers*. Landmark Books, Singapore.

Lee Kip Lin, 1988. *The Singapore house, 1819 – 1942*. Times Editions, Singapore.

Liu, G., 2000. *Singapore, a pictorial history 1819 – 2000*. Archipelago Press, Singapore.

Makepeace, W., G. E. Brooke & R. St. J. Braddell, 1921. *One hundred years of Singapore*. 2 vols. Reprinted 1991, Oxford University Press, Singapore.

National Heritage Board [Singapore], 2002. *Singapore's 100 historic places*. Archipelago Press, Singapore.

Siddique, S., 2000. *Nutmeg, and a touch of spice: the story of Cairnhill Road*. Sembawang Properties, Singapore.

Singh, R., 1995. *A journey through Singapore*. Landmarks Books, Singapore.

Song Ong Siang, 1923. *One hundred years of the Chinese in Singapore*. Reprinted 1983, Oxford University Press, Singapore.

Thomson, J.T., 1864. *Glimpses into life in Malayan lands*. Reprinted 1991, Oxford University Press, Singapore.

Wallace, A. R., 1869. *The Malay Archipelago*. Reprinted 1986, Oxford University Press, Kuala Lumpur.

# Author's Note

The author of these letters is a young British man, as I was too when first I visited Singapore and Malaysia. And the great majority of people mentioned here by name, historical characters, are also Europeans. For it was these who left us records of their lives which are accessible today. So while I hope that the letters are truthful to their times, and nowhere contradict known facts, the truth presented is a partial one. It was not Raffles and Coleman, Butterworth and Dunman who built Singapore but rather the countless Chinese, Malays and others who laboured just as hard but of whose lives we have no record.

For access to the world of Singapore in the mid Nineteenth Century I am particularly indebted to the *Oxford in Asia* reprints which have made so many fascinating contemporary accounts available to today's readers. The sources I judge most valuable are listed above.

I am most grateful to Hazel Marshall and Adrian Foote for commenting on a draft of the book, to the publisher Goh Eck Kheng for his enthusiastic support throughout, and to Lim An-Ling for illustrating the letters exactly as Ben Cook would have wished. Finally, my deepest debt is to Tuck-Chee Phung, now and always.

# Postscript

*John Bastin*

Nineteenth century Singapore cannot be said to be over-supplied with historical materials. There are official records, of course, as well as local and other newspapers; but primary sources, printed and manuscript, relating to individuals are relatively few in number. They also tend to concentrate around the middle years of the century. John Turnbull Thomson's *Some Glimpses into Life in the Far East* (1864) and its *Sequel* (1865) contain amusing anecdotes of colonial life in the Straits, based on his experiences as Government Surveyor between 1841 and 1853. His watercolour and other drawings of the period, like those of Charles Andrew Dyce in the National University of Singapore Museums, made between 1842 and 1847, also provide the first adequate pictorial representations of Singapore.

The latter part of Munsyi Abdullah's *Hikayat* (1849) devotes particular attention to Singapore down to 1846, which is also the starting point of the little known account by V. Fontanier of the five years he spent in Singapore as French Consul, *Voyage dans l'Archipel Indien*. The book was published in Paris in 1852, and in that year Charles Walter Kinloch passed through Singapore on his way to Java, and left us with a pictorial and written account, *Rambles in Java and the Straits in 1852* (1853). Two years later, the British naturalist Alfred Russel Wallace arrived in Singapore for the first time, and his impressions, recorded in his Journal and private letters, provided the basis for the account of Singapore contained in his book, *The Malay Archipelago* (1869).

Actually, his letters, later published in his autobiography, *My Life* (1905), and in James Marchant's biography, *Alfred Russel Wallace* (1916), contain relatively little important information on Singapore. But they are at least something, for personal letters written from Singapore during the nineteenth century are a rare commodity. This has prompted Adrian Marshall to supply the deficiency by writing his own under the pseudonym of 'Ben Cook'. They are based on a number of the above sources, and on Charles Burton Buckley's *Anecdotal History of Old Times in Singapore* (1902). The letters are cleverly conceived and present an authentic view of life in Singapore in 1854-5, as well as describing such dramatic events as the Chinese Riots and the Commission of Enquiry into the affairs of Rajah Sir James Brooke of Sarawak.

Dr. Marshall and his publisher have played fair with their readers by pointing to the modern origin of Ben Cook's correspondence; but the letters are so good that it is interesting to think how they would have been received if they had been published anonymously. They might, perhaps, have matched the success of the hoax played by Abraham Hale in publishing in 1902, under the celebrated imprint of the Oriental printers and publishers, E. J. Brill of Leiden, *The Adventures of John Smith in Malaya 1600-1605*, which has taken in more than one reader over the years. So far as the present letters are concerned, they should be read for enjoyment and with no little admiration for the author's literary and historical skills.

*About the Author*

Adrian G. Marshall was born in Scotland and brought up there and in England, first visiting Malaysia and Singapore in 1966 to undertake research for his PhD on rainforest insects. His subsequent work at the University of Aberdeen has allowed him to revisited both countries many times, as a teacher and researcher in tropical biology, as Co-ordinator of the Royal Society's South-east Asian Rainforest Research Programme and Founding Editor of the *Journal of Tropical Ecology*, and most recently as International Director concerned with student recruitment. Since 1995 he has worked part-time for the university, solely as International Director, and this has allowed him to pursue his interest in Victorian naturalists and explorers in South-east Asia. He lives in Aberdeen with his Malaysian-born partner.

*About the Artist*

Lim An-ling was born in Singapore into an art-loving family. Her formal art training began in 1992 at Nanyang Academy of Fine Arts in Singapore where she majored in traditional oil painting and was first introduced to other arts media. After working as a graphic artist for some years, she travelled to Scotland to study animation at Edinburgh College of Arts, attempting to apply her varied skills to moving pictures. Her interest in art is broad, and travelling has definitely helped to widen her artistic perceptions. She particularly wishes to thank her father for sharing with her his fascinating views and memories of Singapore landmarks, past and present.

Text © Adrian G. Marshall, 2004
Illustrations © Lim An-ling, 2004

Published by
Landmark Books Pte Ltd
5001, Beach Road, #02-73/74, Singapore 199588

ISBN 981-3065-77-X

Printed by Tien Wah Press